ESSENTIAL
CUBA

Contents

BEST THINGS TO DO

56 – 71

EXPLORING...

72 – 185

The essence of...

Countries tend to be defined by their climates and histories, but in Cuba those elements have produced a country that transcends the cliché. Almost nothing remains of Cuba's Amerindians, but all subsequent settlers have left their mark. The Spanish built palaces and churches, the British laid out central Havana, and African slaves brought a culture that is still the vital pulse of Cuba. The barriers to travel, raised after the revolution, are now coming down, allowing visitors to experience the fine historical blend that makes up Cuba's people and architecture, the joys of its climate and some of the Caribbean's most spectacular scenery.

features

Cuba lies just 93 miles (150km) from the Florida shore of mainland USA, and is a mere island hop away from Jamaica, but the island's isolation following the revolution of late 1958 meant that for a long time few visitors ever reached it. Now, as Cuba expands its tourist trade in its quest for much-needed foreign currency, the island is open again and everyone can enjoy one of the most alluring islands in the Caribbean.

Flying into Havana from Europe, the visitor is usually treated to a superb view of Cuba's northern coast. The waters of the Atlantic – all shades from turquoise to a rich, deep blue – come as no surprise, but the marvelous tapestry of greens that forms the countryside, from the light green of sugar cane to the dark greens of the forested hills, is a far cry from the "desert island paradise" of the imagination.

These are the other Cubas – beaches of white sand lapped by the warm waters; ranges of hills, their flanks draped with lush vegetation; swamplands where crocodiles and rare birds are still found; old towns with glorious colonial centers; and fields of sugar cane, tobacco, coffee and lush grass where *guajiros* (farmers) tend the crops and *vaqueros* (cowboys) herd the cattle. Cuba is many lands, each one a fascinating place that will leave a lasting impression on the visitor.

GEOGRAPHY

Cuba is the largest of the Caribbean islands. It is 775 miles (1,250km) long and 20–118 miles (32–190km) wide. There are 2,320 miles (3,735km) of coast and over 4,000 offshore islands.

POPULATION

Cuba has 11 million inhabitants, about 2 million of whom live in Havana. There are an estimated 1.5 million Cuban exiles living in the US, most of them in Florida.

ECONOMY

Tourism is Cuba's largest source of foreign currency, along with sugar, nickel and cigars. "Modern" industries include biotechnology and pharmaceuticals.

In 1959 over 70 percent of Cuba's trade was with the US. After the revolution this evaporated, over 80 percent then being with the USSR. Since the collapse of the Soviet Union, Canada, Mexico, Venezuela and the EU have become Cuba's main trading partners.

PEOPLE

Cuba's native population of Amerindians was wiped out by the Spanish settlers. Today's Cubans are a mix of colonial Spanish and African slaves. Officially the country is 66 percent white, 22 percent mixed race and 12 percent black, but as visitors will soon realize, the terms are easier to define than the differences are to spot.

TOURISM

At present almost 2 million tourists visit Cuba each year compared to the 10 million who visit the Bahamas.

food & drink

Traditional Cuban cuisine is an exciting blend of Spanish and African cooking, which can be difficult to find today, when economic restrictions mean that much of the island's produce is exported to earn foreign currency.

The food served at most tourist hotels is of the type usually labeled "international", often described by the consumers as bland. Things are sometimes a little better in the state-run restaurants and can be much better in the *paladares* (family-run, but state-sanctioned restaurants, usually within a private home). These spring up and close down with a rapidity which defies the possibility of a list being compiled, but are worth seeking out.

COCINA CRIOLLA

Cuba's *cocina criolla* (Creole kitchen) is a basic cuisine, built around providing nourishing food for agricultural workers. The basis will be meat (vegetarians are likely to be frequently disappointed in Cuba), usually pork, but occasionally chicken. Beef is rarely served (even in the tourist hotels), despite the herds of cattle travelers see in central Cuba. If beef is available it will be *picadillo* (minced) or *palomilla* (steak brushed with olive oil and garlic). Meat is usually roasted (*carne asada – puerco asado* is roast pork) or grilled and served with a mix of rice and beans – called *congri* if the beans are kidney

beans, or *moros y cristianos* (Moors and Christians, a reference to the island's own racial mix) if they are black beans.

Rice and beans are also the basis of *potage*, usually served first, a filling mixture of white rice and a thick bean soup. Similar to *potage* is *ajiaco* (sadly not seen often in restaurants), a thick peasant stew of meat and vegetables, flavored with garlic.

For vegetables you will probably be offered a poor seasonal salad, yuca or plantains. Yuca is a native root vegetable which is boiled or baked.

Plantain is a cooking banana and is usually served as *maduros* or *tostones*. For *maduros* slightly sweeter plantains are lightly fried. *Tostones* is one of Cuba's specialties – plantains cut into thick strips, fried, then flattened and refried.

As for dessert, export means that very little of the usual Caribbean fruit finds its way to market and menu. However, Cuban ice cream *(helado)* is excellent. If it is not on the menu, look for the Coppelia ice-cream parlor – every town has one.

WHAT TO DRINK

Cubans start the day with coffee. A *café Cubano* (also known as *cafecito* or *mezclado*) is served in a small cup and is very black and strong. The Cubans lessen the impact with spoonfuls of sugar. After a meal it is better to go for a *café con leche*, that is "with milk". *Café americano* is the same thing.

Sodas are widely available, as are packaged fruit juices and, less so, *guarapo* (sugar cane juice).

All Cuban beers are lager. The most popular is Cristal, which is not as strong as Bucanero. Hatuey, Polar and Tinima are other popular brands.

For spirits drinkers, Cuba means rum *(ron)*. It comes in three-, five- and seven-year *(tres, cinco or*

siete años) forms, the youngest being the cheapest. Basic rum is "white" (colorless), but can be made to darken by storing in oak barrels or adding caramel. Rum is also the basis of Cuba's numerous cocktails. The *mojito* and *daiquirí* are the most famous, but the *Cubanito* (a rum bloody Mary) and the *Cuba Libre* (rum and cola) are equally popular.

ON THE ROCKS

A *mojito* is made from rum, soda water, lime juice, sugar and mint, and a *daiquirí* from rum,

sugar, lime and crushed ice. The latter has a much debated history. Did U.S. troops find the locals making the drink when they landed at Daiquirí Beach during the Spanish-American War? Or was it invented by a miner at the Daiquirí copper mine near Santiago? The only certainty is that a real Cuban *daiquirí* is nothing like the cocktail you will buy elsewhere.

THE ESSENCE OF CUBA

If you only have a short time to visit Cuba, and would like to sample the very best that the country has to offer, here are the essentials:

● **Visit a Casa de la Trova.** Every town and sizeable village has such a house. Here local bands will play traditional songs, such as *son.*

● **Visit a revolutionary site.** Visitors arriving at Havana's José Martí Airport are greeted by the slogan *Creemos en la Revolución* – We believe in the revolution. To understand Cuba the visitor must understand the 1959 revolution.

● **Buy a T-shirt.** Cuban T-shirts, especially those decorated with revolutionary slogans or pictures of Che Guevara, are a distinctive and attractive souvenir.

● **Visit a site on the Hemingway Trail.** Most of the best works by one of the century's most influential writers were written in Cuba. His house is the target for true pilgrims, but even casual readers can pay homage at La Bodeguita del Medio (➤ 77) or El Floridita (➤ 114).

● **Visit a cigar factory.** Cuban cigars are still the world standard. Even non-smokers will find a visit fascinating.

● **To gain an insight into the real Cuba,** try visiting Cárdenas if you are staying in Varadero, or visit Baracoa (➤ 36–37) if you are in Guardalavaca or Ciego de Ávila if you are in Cayo Coco.

● **Go for a swim.** You haven't experienced Cuba until you have submerged yourself in the warm, turquoise waters of the Atlantic or Caribbean.

● **Sample a Cuban ice cream.**
Food is rationed in Cuba and as a result often disappointing, but the island still has wonderful ice cream. Try the coconut or mango flavors.

● **Take a stroll through Old Havana.**
No trip would be complete without a visit to this magical quarter.

● **Visit a cabaret** to savor the louche carry-over from the 1950s. Havana's Tropicana revue (► 109) is Cuba's sexiest cabaret.

Planning

Before you go

WHEN TO GO

JAN	FEB	MAR	APR	MAY	JUN	JUL	AUG	SEP	OCT	NOV	DEC
26°C	26°C	27°C	29°C	30°C	31°C	32°C	32°C	31°C	29°C	28°C	26°C
79°F	79°F	81°F	84°F	86°F	88°F	90°F	90°F	88°F	84°F	82°F	79°F

High season   Low season

February to April are the most pleasant months to visit, weatherwise, while the summer months are hot and humid, often with storms. Mid-winter months are also usually clear and warm; these are the business months. June through November is the hurricane season. The temperatures given above are the average daily maximum for each month in Havana.

WHAT YOU NEED

● Required
○ Suggested
▲ Not required

	UK	Germany	Canada	Netherlands	Spain
Passport valid for 6 months beyond period of stay	●	●	●	●	●
Tourist Card (holiday travel up to 4 weeks; extensions can be requested for an additional 30 days)	●	●	●	●	●
Onward or Return Ticket	●	●	●	●	●
Health Inoculations	▲	▲	▲	▲	▲
Health Documentation	●	●	●	●	●
Travel Insurance	●	●	●	●	●
Driving Licence (national, but international recommended)	●	●	●	●	●

WEBSITES

Cuban Government
www.cubagob.cu
Hoteles Habaguanex
www.habaguanex.com

Havana Journal
http://.havanajournal.com
Ministry of Tourism
www.cubatravel.cu

TOURIST OFFICES AT HOME

In the UK
Cuba Tourist Board
154 Shaftesbury Avenue
London WC2H 8HL
☎ 020 7240 6655
www.travel2cuba.co.uk

In Germany
Cuban Tourist Board
Kaiserstrasse 8
Frankfurt D-60313
☎ 069 288322
www.cubainfo.de

In Canada
Cuban Tourist Board
1200 Bay Street
Suite 305, Toronto
Ontario M5R 2A5
☎ 0416 362 0700
www.gocuba.ca

HEALTH INSURANCE
Medical insurance is compulsory, though the cost of treatment is low in comparison to North America and Europe. Resorts and major cities have international clinics specifically catering to tourists; only basic services are available in many other areas. Health services are excellent, indeed arguably the best in Latin America, but lack of money often means medicines are not available. Note that visitors admitted to hospital are likely to be tested for HIV/AIDS as a matter of routine and may be deported if found to be a carrier.

TIME DIFFERENCES

GMT	Cuba	Germany	USA (NY)	Netherlands	Spain
12 noon	7AM	1PM	7AM	1PM	1PM

Cuban local time is the same as Eastern Standard Time in the US, which is 5 hours behind Greenwich Mean Time (GMT–5). Clocks are turned forward an hour in late March/early April and back an hour in late October.

NATIONAL HOLIDAYS

1 Jan *New Year's Day*
1 May *International Labor Day*
26 Jul *Assault on the Moncada Barracks*
10 Oct *Start of First War of Independence*
25 Dec *Christmas Day*

In addition, there are "unofficial" holidays on 31 December, 25 July and 27 July. There are also a large number of other significant days (such as the birthday of José Martí on 28 January, Bay of Pigs Victory on 19 April, and so on) when some or all official shops and offices will close.

WHAT'S ON WHEN

A useful website for Cuba's festivals and events is www.cubaabsolutely.com.

January *New Year:* Cubans have a traditional meal formerly held at Christmas. It is also the anniversary of the revolution.

José Martí's Birthday (28 Jan): Cultural events celebrate Martí's birthday. The Varadero Carnival starts in late January with events continuing into February.

February *Celebrations of the Second War of Independence* (24 Feb).

Havana Cigar Festival: in Havana.

March 13 Mar: Events to celebrate the attack on the Presidential Palace in 1957.

April *Celebration of the Bahía de Cochinos (Bay of Pigs) victory* (19 Apr).

Bienal de la Habana: Hundreds of artists from more than 40 countries exhibit across multiple galleries, spaces and streets throughout Havana. The next *Bienal* will be in 2012.

May *May Day Parade:* The parade assembles from 6am; the march lasts from 9am to about midday. Anyone can join and parade past the dignitaries (including Raúl Castro) in the Plaza de la Revolución.

Romería de Mayo (3 May): Pilgrimage to Loma de la Cruz, Holguín. Bands and orchestras play in the town squares.

Ernest Hemingway International Marlin Fishing Tournament: at Marina Hemingway, in the west of Havana.

June *Fiestas Sanjuaneras:* in Trinidad, the town's carnival.

July *Carnival:* in Santiago de Cuba. Also a carnival in Havana.

Martyrs of the Revolution (26–28 Jul): Events nationwide.

August *Symposia de Hip Hop Cubano:* Cuban hip-hop has been flavor of the month for the last few years. It's officially celebrated through this annual festival held in Vedado, the cultural heart of Havana, at the Casa de la Cultura de Plaza, at Calzada and Calle 8 (third week in August).

September *Festival Internacional Teatro:* A biennial festival of theater in Havana (late Aug–early Sep).

October *Death of Che Guevara* (8 Oct): Events to remember Che's death in Bolivia in 1967.
Anniversary of the start of the First War of Independence in 1868 (10 Oct).
28 Oct: Children throw flowers into the sea in memory of revolutionary Camilo Cienfuegos, who died in a plane crash in 1959.
Festival Internacional de Ballet (late Oct–early Nov): biennial ballet festival in Havana under the aegis of the Cuban National Ballet. Havana also hosts a modern music festival in October.

November *Semana de la Cultura* (last two weeks): Cuba's artistic heritage is celebrated in Trinidad.

December *Festival Internacional de Corros* (International Choir Festival): in Santiago de Cuba.
Parrandas in Remedios (► 154).
Festival Internacional de Jazz: In Havana.
Festival of New Latin American Cinema: In Havana.

Getting there

BY AIR

José Martí International Airport, Havana

25 kilometers (15.5 miles) to city center

📟	N/A
🚌	N/A
🚐	45 minutes

Juan Gualberto Gómez Airport, Varadero

12 kilometers (7.5 miles) to resort center

📟	N/A
🚌	30 minutes
🚐	20 minutes

Havana's José Martí International Airport is served by over 20 international airlines. Cuban's own Cubana Airlines flies to 17 destinations worldwide.

Virgin Atlantic (☎ 0844 209-7777, www.virgin-atlantic.com) has scheduled flights from London. Air Europa (www.aireuropa.com), Air France (www.airfrance.com), Iberia (www.iberia.com) and Martinair (www.martinair.com) offer regular scheduled services to Havana. Additional flights serve Holguín, Santiago de Cuba and Varadero, and other regional airports on a less frequent basis.

Air Canada (www.aircanada.com) has daily flights to Havana from Toronto. Several charter companies also offer departures from cities throughout Canada, primarily to Varadero and other regional cities serving Cuba's main beach resorts.

From the US, licensed charter flights offered through Marazul Charters (☎ 305-828-8950 or 1-800-223-5334, www.marazulcharters.com) fly direct to Havana from Miami, Los Angeles and New York for licensed travelers only.

An exit tax of CUC25 must be paid on departure.

Getting around

PUBLIC TRANSPORTATION

Internal flights Cubana flies between all the major towns; their fleet of ex-Soviet aircraft has been replaced by modern French planes. Fares are relatively low and the timetables are generally reliable. However, Cubana's safety record is poor. Cubana's main office is at the bottom of La Rampa (Calle 23) in Havana-Vedado at No 64 e/ P y Infanta (☎ (07) 838-1039).

Trains Cuba is the only Caribbean island with a railway system. All major towns are linked to Havana by rather inefficient services. The main route runs along the length of the island, from Havana to Santiago de Cuba via Camagüey, and this is the route most likely to be of interest to visitors. The trains are inexpensive, if slow and overly air-conditioned, and have some delightful touches, such as the man who brings around a flask of coffee but has no cups. Checking in an hour before departure is vital (☎ (07) 861-4259).

Buses An efficient tourist bus service between main destinations is run by Víazul (☎ (07) 881-1413, www.viazul.com). Tickets can also be bought at tour agencies and at the kiosk at the airport. Bicycles can be carried for a fee. Be sure to check in an hour before departure.

Ferries High-speed catamarans run from the southern port of Surgidero de Batabanó to the Isla de la Juventud (Island of Youth). The hydrofoils leave at 8am, and the trip takes about two hours, with return trips at 11am. Ferries run frequently across Havana Bay, from Old Havana to Casablanca and Regla, for only 50 Cuban centavos each way.

FARES AND TICKETS

There is no central ticket agency in Cuba. Foreign travelers must pay for all tickets in convertible pesos (CUC). Víazul buses cost from CUC6 to CUC51 (Havana–Santiago) one-way and can be booked online. Train fares cost from CUC3 (Havana–Matanzas) to CUC62.50 (Havana–Santiago); you must show your passport when buying tickets.

TAXIS

Official taxis are readily available at hotels (Cubataxi ☎ (07) 855-5555). There are also unofficial taxis plying for hire (usually away from the hotels as they are not allowed near them). The price should be fixed in advance, and they will not take you to beaches or airports, which are heavily policed. It is safe to use them.

DRIVING

- Rental companies provide 24-hour breakdown telephone numbers.
- Drive with extreme caution: foreigners tend to be held responsible for accidents, and jail terms are mandatory for causing injury or death.
- Many roads are very bad in Cuba, and the majority are unsignposted.
- Do not drive at night – unlit vehicles and cyclists make roads hazardous.
- Speed limits are as follows:
  on highways *(autopista)*: 100kph/62mph
  on paved roads: 90kph/56mph
  on dirt roads: 60kph/37mph
  on urban roads: 50kph/31mph (but 40kph/25mph near schools)
- Seat belts are compulsory but are absent from all but the most modern vehicles.
- Random breath tests are allowed, but these are rarely carried out. The blood alcohol limit is 80mg/100ml.
- Fuel comes in two grades: *especial* and *regular*. Both are leaded and as a rule only the pricier *especial* is available to tourists. It is sold at 24-hour Servi-Cupet and Oro Negro petrol stations for CUC only. Locals use these stations (if they can afford to) or their own peso stations (which do not often have fuel). Regular fuel should not be used in hire cars: if it is, hire companies will charge heavily, as it blocks carburettors.
- Do not set out in a car without the *Guía de Carreteras* road map, available in a few locations in Havana.

CAR RENTAL

Rex (☎ (07) 683-0302; www.rex.cu) is one of the best of the limited number of state-run car rental companies, offering a range of vehicles from the budget Daewoo Tico to large Mercedes and Dodge Caravans. Four-wheel-drive vehicles are also available for those contemplating dirt roads. You can rent from one town and drop off at another, but at a price.

Being there

TOURIST OFFICES

Since most tourism to Cuba is packaged, there are few tourist offices, although the main resort and town hotels provide a local service through travel agencies such as Cubatur. The national tourist information network, Infotur, has offices in major destinations, and their offices are a good place to try if you are in need of further information. Try the following branches:

Havana
- Calle Obispo
  (e/ Bernazas y Villegas)
  Old Havana
  ☎ (07) 866-3333
- Calle Obispo
  esq San Ignàcio
  Old Havana
  ☎ (07) 863-6884

Note esq = corner of stated roads
e/ = between stated roads

Varadero
- Infotur
  Calle 13 esq Avenida
  Primera (1er)
  ☎ (045) 662961

Santiago de Cuba
- Infotur/Cubatur
  Calle Heredia esq
  General Lacret
  ☎ (022) 669401/686033

MONEY

There are two currencies in Cuba. Cubans are paid in national pesos (CUP; 1 peso is worth 100 centavos), which has an official exchange rate of 26:1 with the Cuban convertible peso. However, there is virtually nothing of value to buy using national pesos, except street food and goods in farmers markets. Tourists must use convertible pesos (CUC) for most transactions. There are official bureaux de change called Cadeca (found everywhere), which change foreign currency for convertible pesos at around 0.926:1 dollar, 1.47:1 pound, and 1.5:1 euro (but check exchange rates before travel). Convertible pesos can only be converted in Cuba and will be useless if you take them home. US dollars are no longer accepted for direct payment, and a 10 percent surcharge applies to exchanging dollars for convertible pesos. Euros are accepted in hotels and restaurants in Varadero, Cayo Coco and Cayo Largo.

TIPS/GRATUITIES

Yes ✓   No ✗

Restaurants and cafes	✓	5–10%
Bars	✓	change
Taxis	✓	round up bill
Porters	✓	CUC1
Chambermaids	✓	CUC1
Museum/tour guides	✓	coins
Car park attendants	✓	CUC1–2
Musicians	✓	CUC1

POSTAL AND INTERNET SERVICES

Cuba has very few official mail boxes, so tourists are best advised to mail their letters and postcards at a hotel or at the airport. Even so, mail delivery is erratic, with letters taking anything up to a month to reach Europe. There is no *poste restante* service, but your hotel may oblige.

Every city now has internet service, including at *telepuntos* (telephone exchanges) and at major post offices. Most tourist hotels also have cybercafes, with prices starting at CUC5 per hour (the more expensive the hotel, the more expensive the service).

TELEPHONES

Cuba's telephone system is being updated, but can be a cause of

frustration. Card phones (buy cards in hotels or at ETECSA offices), are now common in all major cities and can be used to direct dial abroad at CUC1.50 per minute to the U.S., or from CUC1.80 per minute to Europe. Phoning from a hotel will be expensive. All major towns have a *centro telefónico* with booths. You are unlikely to be allowed to make a collect call, as Cuba wants to earn hard currency from your call. To make an international call from your hotel room add the prefix 88, and from a card phone add 119.

International dialing codes
From Cuba dial 00 followed by
UK: 44
Germany: 49
USA/Canada: 1
Spain: 34

Emergency telephone numbers
Police: 106
Fire: 105
Ambulance: 106

EMBASSIES AND CONSULATES

UK ☎ (07) 214-2200
Germany ☎ 833-2569
Canada ☎ (07) 204-2516

Spain ☎ 866-8025
US Interests Section ☎ 833-3551

HEALTH ADVICE

Dental services Dental care should be covered by your medical insurance. Check that it is before you set off, as you will have to pay for any treatment. The quality of dental services in Cuba is poor.

Sun advice Take due caution even on cloudy days. Bring your own sun cream, as it can be expensive or hard to find on the island.

Drugs If you are on medication take adequate supplies with you as there will be no problem taking them into the country, whereas local supplies may be limited. Pharmacies operate a 24-hour rota but are very poorly stocked. Local ones charge much lower prices than the ones in international clinics, which serve tourists and are well stocked.

Safe water The water supply in most upmarket hotels is excellent, but elsewhere tap water should be treated with caution. Bottled mineral water is recommended and is readily available, but expensive.

PERSONAL SAFETY

Cuba is still the safest place in Latin America, but with the increase in tourism, the crime rate has risen. The most likely target is your hire car, but bag snatching and muggings are also rising in frequency. If this happens to you, don't try to salvage anything. Violent crime is extremely rare – Cubans are just desperate for hard currency. Crime against tourists is treated very severely.

● Avoid demonstrating your comparative wealth, and use any security boxes at your hotel to store valuables, particularly your passport.

- Carry your bag across your chest rather than on your shoulder.
- Avoid dimly lit streets at night; in Central Havana it is advisable to take a taxi at night rather than walk.

ELECTRICITY
Cuba's power supply is 110v AC, 60Hz as in the US, though some hotels offer sockets at 220v as well. New, Spanish-built hotels often use European round-pin plugs instead of the American flat ones, but it can be hard to find this out in advance.

OPENING HOURS

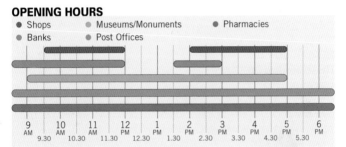

Shop opening times are flexible, depending on whether the shop has anything to sell, but convertible peso shops catering for tourists generally stay open longer. Banks in resorts also tend to stay open longer than 3pm. Post offices in some large towns stay open until 10pm. Pharmacies provide a 24-hour service on a rota basis.

Museum opening times tend to be erratic, particularly for the smaller ones, which may open whenever the curator feels like it. Most are closed on Mondays, and some open on alternate Sundays.

LANGUAGE
Cubans speak Spanish, but with a number of "Cubanisms" which owe their existence to the long years of isolation from Spain and the influence of the African slaves. The pronunciation is Latin American – that is, ce, ci and z are pronounced "s" not "th" as in Castilian Spanish. However, Spanish speakers will have no difficulty in understanding or in being understood. Many young people also speak English. A few useful words and phrases are listed opposite.

yes	*sí*	¿where is... ?	*dónde está...?*
no	*no*	open	*abierto*
please	*por favor*	closed	*cerrado*
thank you	*gracias*	today	*hoy*
hello	*hola*	tomorrow	*mañana*
goodbye	*adiós*	ladies	*damas/mujeres*
good morning	*buenos días*	gentlemen	*caballeros/hombres*
good afternoon	*buenas tardes*	bank	*banco*
good night	*buenas noches*	exchange office	*cambio/Cadeca*
excuse me	*perdón/permiso*	banknote	*billete*
you're welcome	*de nada*	coin	*moneda*
how much?	*¿cuánto?*	travelers' cheque	*cheque de viajero*
do you speak	*¿habla usted*	credit card	*tarjeta de crédito*
English?	*inglés?*	money	*moneda/dinero*
I don't understand	*no entiendo*		*effectivo*
hotel	*hotel*	reservation	*reservación*
bed and breakfast	*dormir y*	with bath	*con baño*
	desayunar	with shower	*con ducha*
single room	*habitación*	with a view	*con vista*
	sencilla	air-conditioned	*climatizado*
double room	*habitación doble*	toilet	*servicio/baño*
one person	*una persona*	lift	*ascensor*
one night	*una noche*	hot water	*agua caliente*
breakfast	*desayuno*	dessert	*postres*
lunch	*almuerzo*	bill	*cuenta*
dinner	*cena*	beer	*cerveza*
waiter/waitress	*camerero/camerera*	wine	*vino*
meat	*carne*	water	*agua*
fish	*pescado*	rum	*ron*
train	*tren*	bus	*ómnibus (gua-gua*
railway station	*estacíon/*		*in 'Cuban')*
	terminal de tren	boat	*barco*
airport	*aeropuerto*	ticket	*boleto*
flight	*vuelo*	car	*coche/carro*

Best places to see

1

Baracoa

Remote Baracoa sits seductively on the Bay of Honey, surrounded by lush tropical vegetation and hidden archaeological sites.

Its forests are home to the smallest bird, frog and bat in the world, and the multicolored polymita snail, whose bright hues reflect the colors of the earth. The forests of royal and coconut palms are protected within the Reserva Biosfera Cuchillas de Toa, centred on El Yunque, a dramatic flat-topped mountain. There are few better places to relax, and legend has it that those who swim in the Río de Miel (River of Honey) will always return to Baracoa.

In October 1492 Columbus landed on the northern coast of Cuba believing he had reached Japan. The exact place of his landing is still disputed – but not by the inhabitants of Baracoa. They have no doubt that Columbus came ashore here, pointing to their most treasured relic, the Cruz de la Parra, as proof. The cross, now in the church of Nuestra Señora de la Asunción in Plaza Independencia, is reputed to have been brought ashore by Columbus and planted on the beach. It was lost for many years, being found among vines (hence the name, the Cross of the Vines). Carbon dating indeed found that the cross dates from the mid-15th century, Columbus' era, but the wood it is made from is indigenous to Cuba. Outside the church stands a statue of Hatuey, the chief of the Amerindians, who put up a strong fight after Diego Velázquez created the first permanent settlement at Baracoa in 1512. When Hatuey was captured, Indian resistance ended. Today he is a hero to the Cubans, who see him as resisting imperialism. The municipal museum in **Fuerte Matachin,** an 18th-century fort – one of three within the town's boundaries – has more on Baracoa's fascinating history.

The **Museo Arqueológico Cueva de Paraíso,** a cliffside cave, contains pre-Columbian relics, including skeletons.

✚ 23L 🍴 Restaurante Duaba ($), Hotel El Castillo; tel: (021) 645-106

Fuerte Matachin

✉ Calle Martí 🕓 Daily 8–noon, 2–6 ✋ Inexpensive

Museo Arqueológico Cueva de Paraíso

✉ Avenida Moncada, 440 yards (400m) south of town

🕓 Mon–Fri 9–5, Sat 9–noon ✋ Inexpensive

2 Catedral de La Habana

Dominating an airy square at the heart of Old Havana is one of the island's most distinctive buildings.

Though it is known "officially" as the Catedral de La Habana, many Cubans refer to it as San Cristóbal. On 15 January 1796 a boat dropped anchor in Havana's harbor and a velvet-draped coffin was rowed ashore. The coffin, believed to hold the remains of Christopher Columbus (Cristóbal Colón), was transferred to the

cathedral. The small lead casket inside contained only a small quantity of dust and a bone fragment, but was laid below a marble slab and became a focus for ceremony. It is now accepted that the remains, which were shipped back to Spain in 1899, were probably those of Columbus' son, Diego.

The cathedral was begun by the Jesuits in 1748, their first task being the draining of an area of swamp. In 1767, with the building still unfinished, the Jesuits were expelled from all Spanish territory by King Carlos III. After a five-year gap, work began again and was completed in 1777. The facade is the finest example of baroque architecture in Cuba. It has been described as the most beautiful in Latin America, and as "music turned to stone". Others find the facade over-elaborate to the point of vulgarity. One curiosity is the two quite dissimilar bell towers, strangely at odds with the otherwise symmetrical facade.

The cathedral's interior is almost austere, having been stripped of much of its finery. Only the altar, with its Carrara marble, onyx and gold and silver inlay, hints at the former treasure once found here. The tower can be climbed for CUC1.

🏠 *La Habana 7b* ✉ Plaza de la Catedral 🕐 Mon–Sat 10:30–2 and Sun mornings for Mass, but these times are notoriously erratic ♿ Free 🍴 El Patio ($$$)
ℹ Infotur, e/ Villegas y Bernaza; tel: (07) 866-3333; www.infotur.cu

3 El Cobre

The statue of Cuba's patron saint, the Virgin of Charity, is found in this remote, but exquisite, church.

In 1608 three boys were fishing in Nipe Bay, off the north Cuban coast, when a sudden storm threatened their boat. They noticed something floating by and hauled it in to discover a statue of a mulatto Virgin bearing the inscription "I am the Virgin of Charity," in Spanish. The storm abruptly ended and the boys were safe. Legend has it that the statue – in wood and about 12 inches (30cm) high – was given to a Cuban Indian chief by a Spanish conquistador in about 1510.

The lovely church in Cobre that now houses the statue is Cuba's only basilica and is in a beautiful setting, its cream walls and towers and red domes contrasting with the green hills beyond. It dates largely from a major rebuilding in the 1920s. The Virgin of Charity was declared the patron saint of Cuba in 1916, and the new church was consecrated on the saint's day, 8 September 1927. There is still an annual pilgrimage to the church on that date.

Beside the church are the Stations of the Cross. Inside, stairs lead to a glass case in which stands the statue, clothed in a cloak of satin embellished with gold. There is a remarkable and varied collection of votive offerings from pilgrims. The site is also important to followers of Santería, the "Rule of Saints," for whom the statue represents Ochún,

the goddess of love, whose color is yellow like the Virgin's golden robe.

The negative aspect to El Cobre is the youths trying to sell souvenirs and pyrites.

✚ 20M ✉ Above the village of Cobre, 12 miles (19km) northwest of Santiago de Cuba 🖐 Free, but donations welcome 🍴 Hospedaría de la Caridad ($); tel: (022) 346-246 ℹ Parque Céspedes, Santiago de Cuba; tel: (022) 66-9401

4 Escambray Mountains

Though not the highest mountain range in Cuba, the Sierra del Escambray is aruguably the most beautiful, its purple peaks rising above lush green foothills.

Cuba is not a mountainous country: its highest peak, Pico Turquino in the Sierra Maestra to the west of Santiago de Cuba, rises to just 6,468ft (1,972m), many feet lower than Blue Mountain on the much smaller neighboring island of Jamaica. Escambray is the second highest range, its highest peak, Pico de San Juan, rising to only 3,792ft (1,156m). The peaks are covered in lush rain forest that is home to a remarkable number of plant and animal species.

The Escambray, officially known as the Guamuhaya, can be explored on foot, but a licensed guide is compulsory. Arrange your own guide or join a scheduled tour through Gaviota.

From Santa Clara (▶ 158–160), go south to Manicaragua, then west to the vast reservoir of Lake Hanabanilla. Here boats can be rented to the southern shores, where well-marked trails can be followed into the forest. The most popular area is Topes de Collantes, a mountain resort built originally as a sanatorium for tuberculosis sufferers.

Topes lies about 12.5 miles (20km) northwest of Trinidad and connects with Manicaragua via a scenic mountain road. Now a national park, Topes has several trails that weave through the rain forest to spectacular waterfalls, such as Salto de Caburní. Other trails lead to the Finca Codina coffee estate, which has an orchid garden and easy trails into the forest.

From the resort a badly deteriorated road heads west to La Sierrita, passing close to the high point of Pico de San Juan. The views are spectacular, but a four-wheel-drive vehicle is advisable. The coast road that links Trinidad and Cienfuegos offers fine views from below.

✚ 11D ✉ Between Santa Clara and Trinidad 🍴 El Río Negro ($$) on Lake Hanabanilla or Restaurante Mi Retiro at Topes de Collantes ($$) ❓ Boat excursions are possible on Lake Hanabanilla from the Hotel Hanabanilla ℹ Gaviotatours, Topes de Collantes; tel: (042) 54-0193/0219

5 Malecón, La Habana

On calm days, on stormy days, by moonlight or in the sun, Havana's Malecón offers a superb walk.

Malecón means jetty, the original purpose of the massive construction that runs for more than 3 miles (almost 5km) from the mouth of the Río Almendares to the Castillo de la Punta having been to keep the Atlantic Ocean out of the new city of Havana. There has been a sea wall here for centuries; the present structure is the design of a Cuban engineer named Francisco de Albear, whose 1857 plan was not completed until 1902.

The Malecón carries a six-lane road, but the traffic that once thundered along it is now largely a memory, leaving promenaders in peace to enjoy the hiss of the waves as they retreat from the wall. On calm days the sun sparkles off the sea, lovers stroll arm in arm and fishermen cast their lines from the wall edge. By night, musicians bring out their guitars, and street vendors set up stalls to sell snacks such as freshly roasted nuts.

On stormy days the Atlantic smashes into the masonry, sending spectacular plumes of spray across the road. The facades of the buildings lining the Malecón, particularly along the Centro Habana stretch, are a decaying testament to the power and corrosive nature of the sea, but they are now being extensively, if slowly, restored with help from Spain, Portugal and UNESCO.

If you have limited time, come around sunset and follow the promenade in Vedado, from the memorial to Antonio Maceo (a hero of the Second War of Independence) in the Parque Maceo, to the monument for those who perished on the USS *Maine*, whose sinking sparked the Spanish-American War. On the seaward side you will encounter sociable Cubans and courting couples. Further west, police keep you moving past the Tribuna Anti-Imperialista José Martí and the US Interests Section.

✚ *La Habana 1a–6b* 🍴 Restaurante Castropol, Malecón 107 e/ Genios y Crespo; tel: (07) 861-4864

6 Museo de la Revolución, La Habana

Housed in one of Havana's most sumptuous buildings, this museum is the best place to start exploring the history of the revolution.

In 1913, close to a section of the old city walls, work began on a parliament house for the provincial government. By the time the work was completed in 1920 the building had been taken over by the President. It remained the Palacio Presidencial until 1959, when Fulgencio Batista fled from it as Castro's forces secured the country.

The building, with its eclectic style, has been described as looking like a wedding cake, and you're likely to love its ostentatious grandeur or loathe its vulgarity. Tiffany's of New York created an extravagant interior that matched the ornate exterior, though much of their work has been stripped out.

It is impossible to view everything in one visit, but there are items that should not be missed: Che Guevara's black beret; an extraordinary diorama of Che and Camilo Cienfuegos in the Sierra Maestra, the full-size wax models

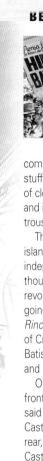

complete with their actual horses, stuffed after death; and a collection of clothing, suitably blood-stained and including Fidel Castro's trousers.

The history of Cuba from its first islanders through Spanish rule to independence is well presented, though the collection of post-revolution statistics is rather hard going. Light relief is offered by *El Rincon de los Cretinos* (the Corner of Cretins) with cartoons ridiculing Batista and US presidents Reagan and Bush.

Outside, on the square at the front of the museum, is the tank said to have been commanded by Castro at the Bay of Pigs. To the rear, visible from the street, is Castro's invasion boat, the *Granma* (► 88), but it can only be viewed at close quarters within the museum.

✚ *La Habana 7b* ✉ Refugio 1 e/ Monserrate y Zulueta ☎ (07) 862 4091 🕐 Daily 10–5 💷 Inexpensive 🍴 None in museum. Café on ground floor of Hotel Sevilla on Prado y Trocadero ℹ Obispo e/ Bernaza y Villegas ☎ (07) 866-3333

Parque Céspedes, Santiago de Cuba

This beautiful and historic park at the heart of Cuba's second city was named in honor of Carlos Manuel de Céspedes.

In October 1868, Céspedes freed the slaves on the sugar plantation he owned near Manzanillo, sparking the First War of Liberation against Spanish rule. Some experts say that a third of a million people died in this bloody, 10-year war and Cuba's sugar industry was virtually destroyed. The war marked the beginning of the end of colonial power: within eight years slavery had been abolished, and within another dozen the Spanish had gone. Céspedes, murdered (while playing chess) at the end of the war, was buried in Santiago.

Parque Céspedes is small and delightfully tree-shaded, and understandably popular with the people of Santiago. On a good day there will be impromptu concerts from local musicians, children playing, animated conversations and people just watching the world go by.

On the Parque's western side is **Casa de Velázquez,** reputedly built by Diego Velázquez, who founded the city in 1515. Much restored, the building is claimed to be the oldest in the whole of Latin America. The first floor has a balcony with a wooden grille, a distinctly Moorish feature. On this floor Velázquez had his offices. Casa Velázquez is now a museum, with some original furnishings and items from Cuba's colonial past. Other equally fascinating buildings flank the square, including the cathedral and the town hall, on the balcony of

which Fidel Castro gave his first speech as Cuba's leader on 1 January 1959.

✠ *Santiago de Cuba 2d* 🚌 Long-distance buses link Santiago to other major cities 🚆 Santiago is on the main cross-island rail line

ℹ️ Infotur, Parque Céspedes; tel: (022) 66-9401

Casa de Velázquez (Museo de Ambiente Colonial Cubano)

✉️ Parque Céspedes ☎ (022) 65-2652 🕐 Sat–Thu 9–5, Fri 1–5 💰 Inexpensive 🍴 Café La Isabelica ($) in Plaza de Dolores

8 Península de Zapata

As with many other islands, Cuba is rich in endemic plants and animals, and Zapata is the showcase site for these.

The Spaniards named the swampy peninsula to the west of the Bahía de Cochinos (Bay of Pigs ➤ 122) after its likeness to a shoe *(zapato)*. Underlying it is a sheet of limestone, barely above sea level: the

swamp is flooded during the wet season, and in long dry periods a layer of peat is exposed which moves when walked on. Hardwood forests once flourished; charcoal burning has thinned these and some logging is still allowed, but at the western tip of Zapata a National Park has been set up to protect the wilderness.

Around 90 percent of Cuba's bird species can be found on the peninsula, including flamingos and the bee hummingbird, the world's smallest bird. The rare Zapata wren and Zapata rail occur nowhere else on earth. The wren, an inconspicuous grayish-brown bird, has a fine song. The rail is sometimes heard by lucky visitors, but the bird is seldom seen – even by those studying it.

Zapata is home to the Cuban crocodile, once on the verge of extinction (in part because of hybridization with the more common American crocodile) but now bred in a special breeding center. The peninsula is one of the last strongholds of the West Indian manatee, the rarest type of this large, slow-moving aquatic mammal.

Sightseeing trips into the swamp are possible when accompanied by official guides – information

and permits are available from the National Park Office in Playa Larga (☎ (045) 98-7249). Avid bird-watchers should go to the Santo Tomás reserve west of Playa Larga at the head of the Bay of Pigs, or the Las Salinas reserve on the western side of the bay.

🞤 7–8D 🖂 To the west of the Bay of Pigs 🍴 Hotel Guamá ($$), Caleta Buena ($$) 🚌 Two GuamáBusTour buses daily from Jagüey Grande reach Playa Larga. Daily buses link Playa Larga and Playa Girón but service is unreliable 🛈 Tours of some reserves are available daily from the Park Office; expensive

Trinidad

With its narrow, cobbled streets, red-tiled houses and delightful main square, Trinidad is the pearl of Cuba.

On Christmas Day 1514, on the orders of Diego Velázquez, a Mass was held on the site of Cuba's third *villa* (garrison town), and Velázquez named the site after the Holy Trinity (Santísima Trinidad). The town's position, shielded from the rest of Cuba by the Escambray Mountains, meant that smuggling was a profitable activity, adding to the wealth of the local sugar mills and resulting in the beautiful buildings that still stand today. In 1988 UNESCO proclaimed Trinidad a World Heritage Site.

Unusually for Cuban towns, Trinidad was not laid out on a grid, the builders preferring to organize the

streets so that one side was always in the shade. At the heart of the old town is Plaza Mayor. The open park is the sunniest spot in town, the tall palms offering little shade. The roads around the square – and elsewhere in town – are cobbled and closed to traffic, so visitors are free to enjoy the sights as life was lived two centuries ago. On the northeastern side of the square is the late 19th-century Church of the Holy Trinity, in Romanesque style. Also on the square are exquisite colonial buildings, some of which house excellent museums. The **Museo de Arquitectura Colonial** explores Trinidad's history; the **Museo Romántico** has a magnificent collection of late 18th- and early 19th-century furnishings and furniture; and the Museo de Arqueología Guamuhaya explores Cuba's Indian past and natural history.

✚ 11E 🍽 Paladar La Estela ($$) at Bolívar 557. Serves Cuban food in a beautiful colonial courtyard 🚌 Trinidad is linked by daily buses to Havana, Cienfuegos, Santa Clara, Santiago de Cuba and Sancti Spíritus
Museo de Arquitectura Colonial
✉ Calle Ripalda 83 🕐 Sat–Thu 9–5 ✋ Inexpensive
Museo Romántico
✉ Calle Echerrí 52 🕐 Tue–Sun 9–5 ✋ Inexpensive

10 Viñales

Known for its dramatic limestone formations, the Viñales valley is Cuba's most beautiful region, as well as its leading center for tobacco production.

Deep in the heart of the Sierra de Órganos mountains, in Pinar del Río province, the broad Viñales valley is framed to all sides by *mogotes* – soaring, sheer-sided limestone formations (many of them free-standing) that lend inordinate drama to the physical landscape. This landscape – known as karst – can be found all over the world, notably in Puerto Rico, Jamaica, Croatia and China's Guangxi province. *Mogotes* means "haystacks," a fitting description for the formations – the remnants of a limestone plateau that rose from the sea some 160 million years ago during the Jurassic age.

Crowned by riotous foliage and riddled with caverns, these rugged convex-topped hillocks provide adventure aplenty for rock climbers and spelunkers. Cueva del Indio can be explored on foot and by boat on its underground lake. Another cave hosts a cabaret. A third features a replica of a pre-

Columbian village, recalling days when many of the caverns were occupied by Taino Indians and, later, by runaway slaves. Farther west, the Mogote Dos Hermanos (Two Brothers Mogote) is painted with a gaudy mural of the evolutionary journey from amoeba to *Homo sapiens*.

Adding another dimension, this spectacularly scenic vale is famous as a center of tobacco production. Ox-drawn plows till the fields and the clip-clop of horses' hooves echoes down the streets of Viñales, a sleepy rural community with aged tile-roofed, pine-shaded homes that cast visitors back over a century. Three excellent hotels and several dozen *casas particulares* (private room rentals) cater to visitors who wish to steep themselves in the heady atmosphere. Many farmers are happy to welcome you into their fields to teach you about tobacco production, and into thatched curing sheds where harvested leaves are hung to dry and age on long poles.

🔀 4C ✉ 130 miles (210km) west of Havana 🍴 Casa de Don Tomás ($$), in Viñales village, is a restored wooden structure; musicians perform 🚌 Regular Víazul buses to Viñales from Havana

ℹ Centro de Visitantes, Viñales; tel: (08) 79-3157

Best things to do

Great places to have lunch

El Aljibe ($$)

Immensely popular with tour groups, foreign businessfolk and Cuba's monied class. This thatched, open-air restaurant serves a delicious house special – roast chicken in orange sauce.

✉ Avenida 7ma e/ 24 y 26, Miramar, Havana ☎ (07) 204-1583

Las Américas ($$–$$$)

This classy restaurant is in the library of the Du Pont mansion, Xanadú, the most historic place in town (▶ 133).

✉ Avenida Las Américas, Varadero ☎ (045) 66-7388

La Cocina de Lilliam ($$–$$$)

This long-standing *paladar* (family-run private restaurant) occupies the delightful garden patio of a home near the Miramar district. Fresh fish and *ropa vieja* (shredded beef) are recommended, accompanied by a cold Cristal beer.

✉ Calle 48, No 1311 e/ 13 y 15, Havana ☎ (07) 209-6514

Palacio del Valle ($–$$$)

Wonderful surroundings and great seafood are the attractions in this neo-Moorish extravaganza that commands panoramic views of Cienfuegos Bay and Punta Gorda (▶ 147).

✉ Calle 37, Cienfuegos ☎ (043) 55-1003

Paladar Estela ($$)

One of the best private restaurants in Cuba, Estela serves superb *criollo* fare, including braised lamb dishes, at fair prices.

✉ Calle Simón Bolívar 557, Trinidad ☎ (041) 99-4329

Restaurante Al Medina ($$)

As the name suggests, Al Medina specializes in Middle Eastern cooking, in an elegant colonial house dedicated to Cuba's Moorish past. The meze combinations are a good deal.

✉ Calle Oficios 12, Old Havana ☎ (07) 867-1041

Restaurante El Morro ($$)
Enjoy tasty *criollo* dishes in this handsome colonial building perched on the clifftop right next to the Santiago's dramatic fortress.

✉ Parque Histórico El Morro, Santiago de Cuba ☎ (022) 69-1576

Restaurante El Templete ($$–$$$)
El Templete is an excellent harborfront gourmet seafood restaurant with plenty of colonial ambience and great service.

✉ Avenida Carlos Céspedes (Avenida del Puerto) esq Narciso López, Old Havana ☎ (07) 866-8807

Las Ruinas ($$)
Lunch in an old sugar mill with striking modern white lines in Havana's best park.

✉ Cortina de la Presa, Parque Lenin, Havana ☎ (07) 644-2721

La Terraza de Cojímar ($$)
The main draw is the associations rather than the food – eat *arroz con bacalao* (salt cod and rice) right where Hemingway ate it.

✉ Calle 152, No 161, Cojímar ☎ (07) 766-5151

Top activities

Baseball: A spectator sport seems an odd choice as an activity, but Cuban enthusiasm for the sport makes it an absorbing and breathless occasion.

Birdwatching: Anywhere away from the towns will do, but the uplands (especially the Sierra del Escambray ➤ 42 and the Zapata Peninsula ➤ 50–51) are best.

Cycling: With so little traffic this is the ideal way of getting around, but obstacles are many and extreme caution is required.

Deep-sea fishing: Follow in Hemingway's wet footprints and hunt for marlin in the "Blue Stream".

Diving: All the resorts offer reef diving. On Cayo Largo (➤ 126–127) there is excellent wreck diving.

Freshwater fishing: More relaxed than its ocean cousin, but largemouth bass offer good sport, especially at Zaza in Sancti Spíritus (➤ 154–155) province.

Horseback riding: Trot along beaches or through the country at Jardines del Rey (➤ 153), Guardalavaca (➤ 176–177) or Viñales (➤ 54–55).

Snorkeling: For those who don't want to dive, much can be seen by snorkeling in the island's warm waters.

Walking: The lack of maps of the island's wild areas can be daunting, but with caution hiking is very rewarding.

Water sports: Almost any water sport can be followed in Cuba, from sailing to water-skiing.

Best nightlife and entertainment

Café Cantante Mi Habana, Havana
Hone your salsa moves in this popular basement club, which often hosts top acts. On weekends it's packed, so arrive early.

✉ Teatro Nacional, Paseo de Martí y Calle 39, Plaza de la Revolución ☎ (07) 878-4275 ◷ Tue–Sat 4pm–4am

Callejón de Hamel, Havana
Every Sunday morning folkloric group Clave y Guaguancó fills this Havana alley with the sound of rumba and Afro-Cuban drumming. The street is a visual delight as the walls have been painted with giant murals by artist Salvador González.

✉ Callejón de Hamel e/ Espada y Aramburu, Centro Habana ◷ Sun noon–3

Casas de la Música, Havana
Spin your reggaeton grooves or your salsa moves on the popular dance floors at Havana's Casas de la Música. Both venues offer matinee sessions too. There's more of a local crowd at the Centro venue. Check the listings at http://promociones.egrem.co.cu.

✉ Casa de la Música Centro Habana, Calle Galiano 225 e/ Neptuno y Concordia ☎ (07) 860-8296
✉ Casa de la Música Miramar, Calle 20 esq Calle 35, Miramar ☎ (07) 204-0447

Casa de la Música, Trinidad
Next to Santissima Trinidad church, a small plaza plays host to rocking salsa bands. Sip a drink in the spectator chairs or stand at the edge of the cobbled dance floor waiting to be whisked on to salsa like a pro. After the salsa band finishes the party continues on the terrace of the Casa itself.

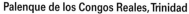 Calle Francisco Javier Zerquera, next to Santissima Trinidad, Trinidad
 Concerts daily from 9pm

Casa de las Tradiciones, Santiago de Cuba

This cramped but authentic music venue is more popular with locals than tourists, and plays host to *son* and salsa bands. It's in the colorful Tivoli section of town.

Calle Rabí 154, Santiago de Cuba ☎ (022) 653-892 Nightly from 10pm

Palenque de los Congos Reales, Trinidad

A small patio plays host to some energetic Afro-Cuban storytelling and dancing in this venue in central Trinidad.

Calle Echerrí, along from Santissima Trinidad, Trinidad Daily

Sábado de la Rumba, Havana

Afro-Cuban dancing, twirling costumes, mesmerizing drumming and solo ballads performed by the Conjunto Folklórico Nacional de Cuba make this an unmissable Saturday afternoon performance.

El Gran Palenque, Calle 4 e/ Calzada y 5ta Avenida, Vedado ☎ (07) 830-306 Sat 3pm

Tropicana, Havana

At Cuba's most fantastical show, semi-clad dancers in feathers and sequins perform exotic and erotic moves under the stars (► 109). Booking is essential, but most hotels can organize the trip for you.

Calle 72 e/ 41 y 45, Marianao ☎ (07) 267-1010 Tue–Sun from 8pm

a walk around Old Havana

Try to start in the early morning to make the most of the cooler hours.

From the southwestern corner of Plaza de la Catedral (▶ 95), go along Calle San Ignacio, turning first left into Calle O'Reilly and continuing to the northwestern corner of Plaza de Armas (▶ 93). Turn right along the square's western edge, then right again along Calle Obispo (▶ 79). Go first left along Calle Mercaderes, passing the Hotel Ambos Mundos (▶ 86–87) and Casa de la Obra Pía, to reach the statue of Simón Bolívar.

The bronze statue was raised to commemorate one of the most famous of Latin American liberators.

Continue along Calle Mercaderes, passing Casa de África on Calle Obrapía (▶ 81) and the Bolívar Museum (No 160). At Calle Brasil, turn right to Plaza Vieja (▶ 96). Cross to the bottom left corner and turn right along Calle Muralla. Go first left along Calle Cuba to see the restored Convento de Santa Clara.

The **church and convent of Santa Clara,** founded in 1638, is now the headquarters of the team restoring Old Havana. The delightful cloisters can be visited.

*Return along Calle Cuba, and follow it northward, crossing Calle Brasil to reach the **Museo Histórico de la Ciencia Carlos J Finlay**, on the left.*

Carlos Finlay discovered that mosquitoes carried yellow fever, and the original site of the Cuban Academy of Sciences was named in his honor. The lecture theater and a 19th-century pharmacy can be visited.

Continue along Calle Cuba, turning fourth right along Calle Obispo, then first left along Calle San Ignacio to return to Plaza de la Catedral.

Distance 1.8 miles (3km)
Time 1 hour's walking, at least 2 more for sightseeing
Start/end point Plaza de la Catedral
🚩 *La Habana 7b*
Lunch Mesón de la Flota ($$) ✉ Calle Mercaderes e/ Amargura y Brasil
Convento de Santa Clara
✉ Calle Cuba e/ Luz y Sol ☎ (07) 861-3335
🕐 Mon–Fri 9–5 💲 Inexpensive
Museo Histórico de la Ciencia Carlos J Finlay
✉ Calle Cuba e/ Amargura y Brasil
🕐 Mon–Fri 8:30–5, Sat 9–3 💲 Inexpensive
🍴 Restaurante Santo Angel ($$$), corner of Plaza Vieja and Brasil at San Ignacio

Great beaches

Cayo Las Jutías

This white-sand beach is close to the beautiful Valle de Viñales.
Away from the small cluster of tourist facilities, walk or take a boat
to admire the huge orange starfish in the shallows.

✉ 37 miles (60km) northwest of Viñales

Cayo Santa María

The isolated set of cays off the coast of Villa Clara is slowly being
developed. The west side of the cays – stretching from Las Brujas
(Isle of Witches) to Santa María – is lined with stunning white-sand
beaches and azure waters (► 148–149).

✉ 46 miles (74km) northeast of Remedios

Guardalavaca

Rolling hills of royal palms tumble down to the rocky coves and inlets of Guardalavaca (➤ 176–177) and nearby Playa Esmeralda. Turquoise and navy blue seas are backed by golden sands and just a handful of hotels. There are interesting Amerindian sites to explore nearby.

✉ 45 miles (72km) northeast of Holguín

Playa Pilar

Undeveloped Playa Pilar unfurls at the western end of Cayo Guillermo (➤ 153). Clouds scud across the blue skies and untainted sand stretches out into a sea of many shades of blue. Cayo Media Luna can be spotted in the distance and is a good snorkeling point.

✉ 13 miles (21km) east of Havana

Playa Santa Lucía

This remote beach area north of Camagüey is known for its excellent diving rather than its beauty. One exciting option is swimming with bull sharks near a boat wreck.

✉ North of Camagüey

Playas del Este

Less than half an hour away from Havana, the glorious white sands of Playas del Este beckon Habañeros and tourists alike. The most beautiful spot is Santa María del Mar, and this is where the principal tourist services are based.

✉ 13 miles (21km) east of Havana

Varadero

Cuba's most famous beach stretches 14 miles (23km) along the Hicacos peninsula (➤ 133). The silky golden sands front a turquoise blue sea that shelves into very shallow, bathtub-warm water. Water sports and other sports facilities abound.

✉ 90 miles (145km) east of Havana

Places to take the children

Cuba may not be riddled with theme parks and funfairs, but the beautiful beaches are ideal for family holidays. All the larger resort hotels offer equipment – and often tuition – for water sports, and can also arrange other activities, such as horseback riding.

Acuario Nacional
Watch sea lions and dolphins perform (➤ 96), or dine next to the enormous dolphin tank in the Gran Azul restaurant.

Ballet Folklórico Cutumba
This extraordinary folkloric group performs mesmerizing dance shows in Santiago.
✉ Former Cine Galaxia, Calle Trocha esq Santa Ursula, Santiago de Cuba
☎ (022) 65-5173; www.cubanfolkloricdance.com

Cueva del Indio
This cave system in the Viñales valley, believed to have been used by Amerindians, makes a good break from the beach (➤ 54).
✉ 4 miles (6km) north of Viñales village ⏰ Daily 9–5

Cuevas de Bellamar
These popular caves near Varadero are very accessible, and a shop, restaurants and playground are all on site too (➤ 120).

Parque Coppelia
The largest ice-cream parlor in the world, Havana's Coppelia takes up an entire block. It has multiple indoor rooms, plus three open-air sections shaded by stately jagüey trees. Locals pay in national pesos but tourists' CUCs are welcomed.
✉ Calle L y 23, Havana ☎ (07) 832-3450 ⏰ Tue–Sun 10–10

Teatro Guiñol
Havana's Guiñol Theater stages children's theater and puppetry.
✉ Calle M e/ 17 y 19, Vedado ☎ (07) 832-6262

Teatro-Museo de Títeres El Arca

Havana's shadow puppet theater appeals to all ages.

✉ Avenida del Puerto y Obrapía ☎ (07) 864-8953

Varasub

This will be an adventure for most children. The Varasub is a surface boat with underwater seats and portholes allowing passengers a close-up view of the sea life near the reefs of Varadero. Reservations can be made at most hotels in Varadero and Havana, at the Tour and Travel stands in Varadero and Havana, or through Havanatur.

✉ Hotel Paradiso, Varadero 🕐 Six trips daily, each lasting 1.5 hours

Stunning views

Castillo de los Tres Reyes del Morro (Havana, ➤ 102–103) View over La Habana Vieja, the Malecón, and Vedado.

Monumento José Martí (Havana) Looking over Plaza de la Revolución (➤ 90) and the entire city from Havana's highest point.

Salón Turquino (Havana, ➤ 116) This nightclub, atop the Tryp Habana Libre hotel (➤ 111), has a great view of Havana by night.

Puente Bacunayagua (Matanzas province) A 1,027ft-tall (313m) bridge with stupendous views over a deep canyon and south towards the Valle de Yumurí.

Las Américas (Varadero, ➤ 58) Superb view along Varadero beach from this historic mansion-turned-restaurant.

From the top floor of the Jagua hotel (Cienfuegos, ➤ 161) south over the Palacio del Valle and Bahía de Cienfuegos.

Antiguo Convento de San Francisco de Asís (Trinidad) Look down over Trinidad and toward Playa Ancón and the Sierra del Escambray.

Loma de la Cruz (Holguín) The highest point for miles (➤ 179) offers sweeping 360-degree views of Holguín province.

Castillo del Morro (Santiago de Cuba)
Magnificent views west along the rugged coastline and north over Santiago de Cuba bay. Best enjoyed at dusk.

El Castillo (Baracoa, ➤ 36–37) Historic hilltop fortress overlooking the ancient city and silvery bay, with El Yunque mountain beyond.

Exploring

Cuba is extremely diverse, and larger than most visitors imagine. The isle is astoundingly pretty. Sugar-fine sands dissolve into peacock blue and green seas, especially along the north shore and Cayo Largo. The Caribbean and Atlantic frame verdant mountains full of emerald-green valleys where ox-drawn plows till the earth. First-time visitors should stick to the highlights, stopping at least a day or two in each chosen key destination. A perfect circuit would take in the Valle de Viñales, plus Trinidad, and a prime beach resort such as Cayo Coco. The route also weaves in the Sierra del Escambray, Santa Clara (for the Che museum) and Varadero. In the east, Santiago de Cuba makes a great base for a circuit through Bayamo, Holguín and Baracoa. For beach time, add a sidetrip from Holguín to Guardalavaca, while Camagüey enchants with its colonial buildings painted in tropical ice-cream colors.

La Habana and around

Starting as a collection of wooden huts beside a natural harbor, La Habana (Havana) rapidly grew to be the jewel in Europe's New World crown. The Havana of the *conquistadores* was an opulent city that reflected the glories of Spain. The wealth of the sugar trade, built on the backs of African slaves, maintained Havana's fortunes.

La Habana

With the end of colonial rule it became a wealthy and glitzy city, with casinos controlled by US gangsters, and a playground for the rich. In the years of economic struggle that followed the events of 1958 the city lost its shine, but its inaccessibility gave it a mystical air, of a once proud city in decline. Now Havana is open again, and the myth is justified. Despite the decay, Old Havana is as gracious as was claimed, with a renovated colonial core as glorious as any in Latin America.

There are two main parts to Havana city center: La Habana Vieja (Old Havana) built by the Spanish in the 16th and 17th centuries; and the newer Centro Habana (Central Havana), built in the 18th century to a design of the British. In 1982 UNESCO declared Old Havana a World Heritage Site and the Cuban government began restoration. Now Old Havana is not only a city of staggering beauty, but one of great character. It should be explored at a leisurely pace, taking time to discover its many delightful hidden corners. In contrast, Central Havana is a more open part of the city, the extra space available beyond the city walls allowing more, and bigger, public spaces.

ASOCIACIÓN CULTURA YORUBA DE CUBA

This museum in Old Havana explains the system of *orishas* (deities) of the Santería faith, which was originally brought to Cuba by Yoruba slaves from West African. They were forbidden to practice their religion, and forced to observe Roman Catholicism, which over time led to the pantheon of Yoruba gods and goddesses becoming syncretized with the Catholic saints. For example, the Virgin of Charity, patron saint of El Cobre, became identified with the *orisha* Ochún, perhaps because both were thought to protect women in childbirth. Today it is thought that as many as 80 percent of Cuba's population practice Santería.

In the museum are 31 *orisha* representations, shown as larger-than-life ceramic statues sitting in a tableau reflecting their identity. Orichaoko, who is the guardian of food and crops, sits in a field of mango and lemon trees; while Olukun, who lives at the bottom of the sea, is represented in a subterranean scene. Visits are accompanied by English-speaking guides who help to explain the characteristics of each *orisha*. There's folkloric dancing between 4 and 7pm every Sunday, and a shop and restaurant on the premises.
www.cubayoruba.cult.cu

🕇 *La Habana 6c* ✉ Paseo de Martí (Prado) 615 e/ Montes y Dragones ☎ (07) 863-5953 🕐 Daily 9–5 🖐 Moderate

LA BODEGUITA DEL MEDIO

Just a short step from the Plaza de la Catedral (➤ 95) is one of Ernest Hemingway's favorite bars. Legend has it that the bar started as a grocery store where writers met at lunchtime. The owner started to serve drinks, then meals, then it opened as a full-time bar in 1942. The B del M (as it is colloquially known) has a decor that is part of its great charm. The walls, ceiling and even the tables are covered in graffiti. The famous names inscribed here include those of such disparate characters as Errol Flynn and Fidel Castro, although most of the original signatures were recently painted over. Pride of place goes to the framed words of Hemingway, "My mojito in La Bodeguita, my daiquiri in El Floridita". There are those who claim the text is fake, an invention by owners anxious to increase trade, but the forgery claim is itself dubious.

🕇 *La Habana 7b* ✉ Calle Empedrado 207 ☎ (07) 867-1374 🕐 Daily noon–midnight

CALLE OBISPO

This is Old Havana's main street, linking the Plaza de Armas with Parque Central. It is traffic free and lined with shops and private galleries, adding art hunting to the delights of the architecture. Heading west from Plaza de Armas, the first gem is El Navío bookstore, No 117–119, built in the mid-17th century and claimed to be the oldest house in the city. With its plant-hung balcony it is a delight. Inside, note the ceilings, which show a distinct Moorish influence. Number 113 houses a small museum of silverware, while at the corner of Obispo and Mercaderes is the Hotel Ambos Mundos (➤ 86–87). Across the street, the formerly ugly Ministry of Education has been rebuilt in dramatic modern brick and glass as a cultural center recalling its origins as the University of Havana, founded in 1728. A stone's throw beyond is the **Museo Farmacia Taquechel,** retaining aged apothecary jars. Farther on toward Parque Central the neo-classical building erected for the Bank of New York is now occupied by the State Finance Company. The former Banco Mendoza, one block west, is now the **Museo Numismático,** displaying coins and banknotes dating back 2,000 years.

✚ *La Habana 7c–8b*

🍴 Cafe Paris ($), Calle Obispo 202

Museo Farmacia Taquechel

✉ Calle Obispo 155 ☎ (07) 862-9286 🕐 Daily 9–5 ✋ Free

Museo Numismático

✉ Calle Obispo e/ Aguilar y Habana ☎ (07) 861-5811

🕐 Tue–Sat 9:30–5:15, Sun 9:30–1

✋ Inexpensive

CAPITOLIO NACIONAL

Visitors who have also been to Washington DC will not be surprised to learn that the Capitolio (Capitol Building) was inspired by the US capital's more famous building. It was ordered by Gerardo Machado, one of the most unsavory of Cuba's list of dictators. Built in the 1920s, it took 5,000 workers over three years to complete and cost $17 million. Entry is through bronze doors whose reliefs represent stages in Cuban history to 1929. Machado's face was destroyed by a mob in the revolution of 1933. Inside, the sumptuous decoration is breathtaking, as is the vast bronze statue of an Amerindian woman representing Cuba. The 24-carat diamond set below the vast dome is the point from which all distances from Havana are measured.

✚ *La Habana 6c* ✉ South of Parque Central ☎ (07) 861-5519 ☺ Guided tours daily 9–5 👤 Inexpensive ❓ Closed for repairs until 2012

CASA DE ÁFRICA

This interesting museum and study center explores Cuba's African heritage and has a collection of African artifacts. There is also the very interesting collection by Fernando Ortíz, a Cuban ethnographer, tracing the origins and beliefs of the Santería cult.

Opposite the museum is **Casa de la Obra Pía,** one of Havana's finest 17th-century buildings, notable for its dramatic baroque portal imported from Spain, for its stained-glass half-moon *mediopuntos*, and for its slave quarters, on the roof. In addition to displays of art, it has some memorabilia of Alejo Carpentier, Cuba's finest 20th-century writer. The building is named for the philanthropy *(obra pía)* of its original owner.

✚ *La Habana 8c* ✉ Calle Obrapía 157 ☎ (07) 861-5798 ☺ Tue–Sat 9:30–4:30, Sun 9:30–1 👤 Free

Casa de la Obra Pía
✉ Calle Obrapía 158 ☎ (07) 861-3097 ☺ Tue–Sat 9–4, Sun 9:30–12:30pm 👤 Inexpensive

CASA DEL ÁRABE

The beautiful 18th-century Colegio San Ambrosio is now a small museum of Islamic culture, with a collection of gifts to Cuba from visiting Muslim leaders and diplomats, with some objects from Spanish/Moorish times. There is a small mosque – the only center for Islamic worship on the island – and a good restaurant specializing in Middle Eastern food (➤ 58).

✚ *La Habana 8b* ✉ Calle Oficios 12 ☎ (07) 861-5868 ☺ Tue–Sat 9–4:30, Sun 9–1 👤 Free

CASA NATAL DE JOSÉ MARTÍ

José Martí, the father of Cuban independence, was born in Havana of Spanish parents in 1853. His Havana birthplace (Casa Natal) is now a museum to his memory, with writings and memorabilia that trace his life. Critical of Spanish colonial rule from his time at school, Martí was imprisoned for treason in 1870, and deported to Spain soon after. Although allowed to return to Cuba after the First War of Independence ended, he was soon arrested and deported again. Finally, in 1895, together with Maximo Gómez, Antonio Maceo and a handful of others, he landed near Baracoa to launch the Second War of Independence, only to be killed early in the war. He is buried at Santiago de Cuba.

La Habana 7d ✉ Calle Leonor Pérez 314
☎ (07) 861-5095 🕓 Tue–Sat 9:30–5, Sun 9:30–1
✋ Inexpensive

CASTILLO DE LA REAL FUERZA

The first fortress on this site was criticized for being ill positioned, a fact French pirates proved conclusively when they destroyed it in 1555. Nevertheless, the Castle of the Royal Force was rebuilt, though after its completion in 1577 it was made redundant by the better-sited fortresses of Cabaña and El Morro (▶ 102). It then became the residence of the Cuban captains general (governors). Today the fortress, still impressively intact, its 9ft-thick (3m) wall rising beyond a moat, houses a collection of shipwreck finds and an extraordinary model of a naval ship. The *castillo* is also famous for La Giraldilla, the bronze

figure of a woman above the westernmost tower. The most popular story says she is Doña Ines de Bobadilla, wife of Hernando de Boto, a 16th-century governor of Cuba who left to seek the Fountain of Youth and never came back. She spent every day for the next four years watching for his return. The figure – actually a replica, the original being in the entrance to the castle – is the official symbol of Havana and can be seen on many souvenirs, everything from postcards to rum bottle labels.

✚ *La Habana 8b* ✉ Plaza de Armas ☎ (07) 861-6130 🕐 Tue–Sun 9:30–5 💵 Inexpensive 🍴 Bar El Cañonazo, Hotel Santa Isabel ($)

CATEDRAL DE LA HABANA

Best places to see, ➤ 38–39.

DESPÓSITO DEL AUTOMÓVIL

This classic car museum displays old motors in a warehouse in Old Havana. While not all the vehicular beauties are explained in the museum, the best-preserved come with notes. The oldest is a model T Ford from 1918, one of only 10 that were imported to kick-start Havana's first cab service. The most luxurious are the gleaming black Cadillac that belonged to Cuba's fourth president, Alfredo Zayas, and a glorious Rolls Royce with upholstered seating and a bonnet mascot of a woman leaning forward in the breeze. Other highlights include a green 1959 Oldsmobile that belonged to rebel Camilo Cienfuegos, a white 1960 Oldsmobile that was driven by Celia Sánchez, Fidel Castro's secretary, and a 1953 black MG driven by one of Cuba's best-loved singers, Benny Moré.

✚ *La Habana 8c* ✉ Calle Oficios 13 e/ Justiz y Obrapía ☎ (07) 863-9942
🕓 Tue–Sat 9:15–5:15, Sun 9:15–1 🚻 Inexpensive

EDIFICIO BACARDÍ

One of the best views of Havana is from the bar on top of the Hotel Plaza near Parque Central (➤ 90–91), but dominating the view is a much nearer building. Built in 1929 by the sugar and rum baron Emilio Bacardí, the Bacardí Building is an extraordinary piece of art deco architecture. Decorated with terra-cotta and (almost) naked nymphs, and topped by a giant version of the company's black bat, the building can certainly claim to be one of the most distinctive in the city.

✚ *La Habana 7b* ✉ Calle Monserrate esq San Juan de Dios

FÁBRICA DE TABACOS PARTAGÁS

There are half a dozen cigar factories in Havana, but only the Partagás factory (near the Capitolio) offers guided tours. To the

disappointment of many visitors, cigars are rolled on wooden blocks rather than on the thighs of beautiful girls, a legendary image for cigar aficionados. Visitors are greeted by the rollers tapping their knives on their tables. A good cigar is made from four leaves: an inner leaf, then the flavor leaf, the combustion leaf that creates an even burn and the outer wrapper, which is glued with rice-glue. The ends are trimmed and, two minutes after starting work on it, the cigar is finished. The factories employ a reader for the rollers, an idea from the earliest days of production to ease the boredom of the work. News and stories are also broadcast on the radio. José Martí was energetic in his efforts to get his anti-colonial pamphlets read at the factories, though romantic novels seemed (and are still) most popular. The factory has a large Casa del Habano (Cuban cigar store) inside.

✚ *La Habana 6c* ✉ Calle Industria 524 ☎ (07) 862-4604 ✪ Factory tours Mon–Fri 9–11, noon–1:30; store Mon–Sat 9–5 💰 Moderate

GRAN TEATRO

The Gran Teatro de la Habana claims to be the oldest theater in the Americas, with a history dating back to 1846, when it opened (as the Teatro Tacón) with a Verdi opera. The claim is more or less true, the Tacón having been bought by a group of Galicians early this century and incorporated into the present structure, a superb albeit crumbling art nouveau building. The theater is home to Alicia Alonso's Ballet Nacional de Cuba, and also offers regular plays and concerts.

✚ *La Habana 6c* ✉ Paseo de Martí (Prado) 452 ☎ (07) 623-410 🕐 Mon–Fri 10–4 👣 Inexpensive 🍴 El Floridita ($$$), ► 114

HOTEL AMBOS MUNDOS

An absolute must for those on the "Hemingway Trail". When Hemingway first moved to Havana he stayed here, in Room 511. The hotel was his home, on and off, until he moved to La Finca Vigía. It is likely that it was here that he wrote the bulk of *For Whom the Bell Tolls*, his classic novel of the Spanish Civil War. The hotel, whose name means "Both Worlds", was built as the elegant mansion of an 18th-century nobleman, though it was enlarged when it became a hotel.

For many years the hotel was left to decay, but a full-scale restoration has been completed, making it one of the best hotels in the old town; open to the street is its lounge, a cool place to relax. Room 511 can be viewed: it is claimed to be as Hemingway left it, but has obviously had to be restored like the rest of the building, though the typewriter, model of his boat, the *Pilar* and whiskey bottle are probably authentic.

✚ *La Habana 7b* ✉ Calle Obispo 153 ☎ (07) 860-9530 🕐 Room 511 open daily 10–5 ✋ Inexpensive

IGLESIA DEL ESPÍRITU SANTO

The original church on this site was built in the 1630s, which has led to the present, larger church that incorporates it being called the oldest in Havana. A Moorish influence is still apparent. The first church was built by freed black slaves, but an interesting sidelight on Cuba's social structure in the 17th century shows that burials – like life – were conducted here on a wealth basis. With grave sites at a premium, the wealthy could buy plots in the nave: those closest to the altar cost most. It is unlikely that any of the ex-slave builders could afford to be buried here. Inside the church there is a statue of St Barbara, equivalent to the god of thunder in the Santería cult.

✚ *La Habana 8c* ✉ Calle Cuba 161 esq Acosta 🕐 Daily 8–noon, 3–6

IGLESIA Y CONVENTO DE SAN FRANCISCO

The earliest church here was built in 1608 (pre-dating that of the Holy Spirit), but the present baroque building is much later. It was a Franciscan monastery, but was later deconsecrated. The church (named for St Francis of Assisi) is now used for concerts. The church's tower was once the tallest in the city and was used as a landmark by approaching ships – and as a lookout in case the ships were pirates.

✚ *La Habana 8c* ✉ Calle Oficios e/ Amargura y Brasil ✋ Inexpensive
🍴 Café del Oriente, Calle Oficios 112 ($$)

MEMORIAL *GRANMA*

The motor boat *Granma*, one of the most potent symbols of the revolution, is displayed adjacent to the Museo de la Revolución (➤ 46–47) and can only be viewed at close quarters by visiting the museum. After the failed attack on the Moncada barracks (➤ 168), Fidel Castro was captured. He was tried and imprisoned on the Island of Youth (➤ 130–131), but released after two years. He went into exile in Mexico, where he was joined by his brother Raúl and Che Guevara. In December 1956 they bought the motor boat *Granma;* 82 revolutionaries packed into the boat and after a storm-tossed crossing during which they were thrown well off course, they landed on Cuba's southeastern coast. Spotted from the air, strafed before they landed and pursued by troops, only a dozen revolutionaries made it to the Sierra Maestra mountains, from where these few launched the successful overthrow of Batista's

regime. Today the *Granma*, neatly but vividly painted, is a national treasure. It is surrounded by other hardware of the revolution – vehicles from the Moncada raid and remnants of a US plane shot down at the Bay of Pigs.

✚ *La Habana 7b* ✉ Behind Museo de la Revolución
🕐 Daily 10–5 💷 Inexpensive

MUSEO NACIONAL DE BELLAS ARTES

Housed in two distinct buildings three blocks apart, the National Fine Arts Museum boasts a world-class collection that includes the finest selection of Cuban art on the island, together with a surprisingly broad and impressive body of works by European and foreign masters. The Cuban collection is displayed in a 1950s building that has been remodeled to show the works in an atmosphere and setting that allow their full appreciation. The homegrown art is chiefly from the 20th century, though there are some works by colonial artists. The 20th-century artists include René Portocarrero, with a style reminiscent of Chagall, and Wifredo Lam, perhaps the Cuban painter best known to outsiders.

The international paintings occupy the elaborate Renaissance-style former People's Supreme Court, on the north side of Parque Central. Occupying five levels, the works are displayed by region (Asian, Europe, Latin America, and the US) and include masterpieces by Turner, Rubens and Canaletto. Also here are antiquities from the Egyptian, Greek and Roman epochs.

www.museonacional.cult.cu

✚ *La Habana 7b* ✉ Calle Trocadero e/ Zulueta y Monserrate (Cuban section), Calle San Rafael e/ Zulueta y Monserrate (International section)
☎ (07) 861-0241 💷 Inexpensive

MUSEO DE LA REVOLUCIÓN

Best places to see, ➤ 46–47.

MUSEO DE RON

Officially the Fundación Destilería Havana Club, the Museum of Rum – housed in a grandiose former mansion of the Conde de la Mortera – does an excellent job of profiling the cycle of rum production, from the growing of sugar cane to the finished product. A highlight is a scale model of a colonial-era sugar cane plantation and processing factory including an electric railroad; and a miniature processing plant with bubbling copper stills produces real rum. The guided tours end in the tasting room and shop, although the prices here offer no discounts.

www.havanaclubfoundation.com

➕ *La Habana 8c* ✉ Avenida San Pedro e/ Muralla y Sol ☎ (07) 861-8051
🕐 Daily 9–5:30 ✋ Moderate

PARQUE CENTRAL

This park was the center of the new Havana designed and, in part, constructed, during the brief period when Cuba was under British rule. Later, after the Prado (➤ 91) was finished, the park became the center of Cuban life. To an extent it still is. At the park's center, standing beneath tall palm trees, is a statue of José Martí, the first such memorial to have been erected in Cuba. It was paid for by public subscription and "unveiled" in the presence of Maximo Gómez, another of the leaders of the Second War of Independence. Martí looks east toward the National Fine Arts Museum (International section, ➤ 89) and Manzana de Gómez, a department store built in 1910. At the time of its construction, and for many years after, it was the finest store in the Americas. Now, greatly dilapidated, it is occupied by a few unimpressive tourist shops.

Behind Martí is the Hotel Inglaterra, with a stunning 19th-century classical facade. The hotel's patio cafe is justifiably popular

with tourists. Beside the hotel is the Gran Teatro (➤ 86). At the northeastern corner of the park is the Hotel Plaza, an excellent hotel with fabulous views of the old town from its top-floor bar.

✚ *La Habana 6c* ✉ Paseo de Martí (Prado) 🍴 Restaurante Anacoana ($$$), Prado esq Dragones

PASEO DE MARTÍ (EL PRADO)

In the late 18th century a new promenade was laid out parallel to the old city walls, its form – and original name – mirroring the Prado of Madrid. Following the revolution, the promenade (about 0.6 miles/1km in length) was renamed the Paseo de Martí though most Habaneros still use the old name. Few buildings on the street are open to visitors, but the whole offers a delightful stroll from Parque Central to the start of the Malecón. On the way, look for the Palacio de los Matrimonios (No 302), once a casino and now a venue for weddings. Farther on, to the right, is the Hotel Sevilla (a short distance along Calle Trocadero), made famous by Graham Greene in his novel *Our Man in Havana*. The area has been renovated.

✚ *La Habana 6b* 🍴 Centro Andaluz ($), Prado e/ Genios y Refugio; Paladar Doña Blanquita ($), Prado e/ Colón y Refugio

PLAZA DE ARMAS

This is Havana's oldest square, and one of the city's finest. A *ceiba* (silk cotton) tree marks the spot where a Mass was held at the founding of the city, and nearby is El Templete, a mock Grecian temple built in 1828 to commemorate the founding. The statue in the square is of Carlos Manuel de Céspedes, instigator of the First War of Independence. On the northern side is the Castillo de la Real Fuerza (► 82–83); the Palacio de los Capitanes Generales, the palace of Cuba's colonial governors and its early presidents is to the western side. It is a beautiful building with elegant balconies and arcades; in the courtyard stands a statue of Christopher Columbus. The *palacio* now houses the **Museo de la Ciudad** (City Museum), displaying outstanding Spanish colonial furniture and objects. As interesting as any item are the lavishly decorated rooms themselves. The (never used) Throne Room, which is undergoing restoration, has a frescoed ceiling and gracious furnishings, while the bathroom features twin large, carved marble bathtubs. Nearby is the Palacio del Segundo Cabo, once the office of the vice-governor and now home to the Cuban Book Institute. On the southern side of the square is the Museo de Ciencias Naturales (Natural History Museum) with its (somewhat tired) collection of Cuba's extraordinary range of flora and fauna.

✚ *La Habana 8b* 🍴 Café La Mina ($$), esq Plaza de Armas y Obispo

Museo de la Ciudad

✉ Palacio de los Capitanes Generales, Plaza de Armas ☎ (07) 861-5779
🕐 Tue–Sun 9:30–5 ✋ Inexpensive

PLAZA DE LA CATEDRAL

The cathedral (➤ 38–39) dominates the square, but is not the only building of interest here. Close to it the **Centro Wifredo Lam** has galleries of contemporary Cuban work and even some foreign artists. On the other side of the cathedral, in the northeastern corner of the square, the Casa de Lombillo, a beautiful *palacio* built in the early 18th century for the Marqués de Lombillo, now houses an exhibition profiling the restoration project of La Habana Vieja. The Casa del Marqués de Arceos, beside the museum, was built at about the same time – and is being restored as a hotel and museum.

Across the square from the cathedral is the plaza's other major building, the Palacio de los Condes de Bayona, begun in the late 17th century but rebuilt in about 1720. It is a magnificent building, with a central courtyard and, upstairs, wooden ceilings. Today it houses the **Museo de Arte Colonial** with a fine collection of furnishings and decorations, mainly European in origin, from Cuba's colonial past. The final side of the square is formed by the Casa del Marqués de Aguas Claras, an elegant building dating from the mid-18th century, which now contains the El Patio restaurant ➤ 114.

➕ *La Habana 7b* 🍽 La Bodeguita del Medio ($$$), ➤ 77

Centro Wifredo Lam

✉ Plaza de la Catedral ☎ (07) 861-2096 🕐 Mon–Fri 10–5 ✋ Free

Museo de Arte Colonial

✉ Plaza de la Catedral ☎ (07) 862-6440 🕐 Tue–Sat 8–5, Sun 9–1 ✋ Inexpensive

PLAZA VIEJA

Glowing anew after a virtually complete restoration, this intimate cobbled plaza is a real charmer, centered on a fountain modeled on the 18th-century original. More spacious and open than Plaza de Armas or Plaza de la Catedral, it also has a more active community presence; Cubans still occupy apartment homes on two sides. Several boutiques, a museum of playing cards, and two fine restaurants – one a brewpub with the brewery open to view – line the square, surrounded by shady columned arcades. The near-derelict, art nouveau Palacio Cueto Hotel is undergoing a lengthy restoration.

➕ *La Habana 8c* 🍴 La Taberna de la Muralla ($), San Ignacio 364

Around La Habana

ACUARIO NACIONAL

Although a little run down, the aquarium still shows visitors the huge diversity of sea life to be found off Cuba's shores. There are also dolphins and sea lions who perform the usual tricks at regular intervals.

www.acuarionacional.cu

➕ *La Habana 1a (off map)* ✉ Avenida 3 esq Calle 62
☎ (07) 230-6401 🕐 Tue–Sun 10–6 ✋ Moderate

CEMENTERIO DE COLÓN

A cemetery seems an unlikely tourist destination, but the Columbus Cemetery is extraordinary – a vast array of ornate sepulchers and gleaming, eye-achingly white sculpture that includes mock temples and castles and even an Egyptian pyramid. Almost every Cuban of importance during two centuries is buried here, from presidents and military figures to revolutionary leaders, sports heroes and artists. The tomb of José Raul

Capablanca, Cuba's world chess champion, is topped by a large chess piece. One of the many legends about the cemetery concerns *La Milagrosa* (the Miracle Worker), Amelia Goyre de la Hoz, who died in stillborn childbirth in 1901. When the grave was opened the child buried at the mother's feet was supposedly in her arms. On the tomb a woman cradles a child in one arm and grasps a cross with the other. Nearby is an array of flowers and messages of gratitude.

✚ *La Habana 1e* ✉ Zapata esq Calle 12 🕐 Daily 8–5 💲 Inexpensive

COJÍMAR

The tiny fishing village of Cojímar's great claim to fame is its association with American writer Ernest Hemingway. Born in 1899, he worked as a journalist before becoming a full-time writer. He was in Spain during the Civil War, then moved to Cuba, where he remained for more than 20 years, only moving when ill health and the deterioration of relations between the US and Cuba made it impossible for him to stay. Shortly after his departure to the US in 1961 he committed suicide.

Hemingway loved fishing, and he had a 40ft (12m) boat named *Pilar* for the patron saint of Zaragoza, which he used to fish for blue marlin, the largest and bravest of the Caribbean's great game fish; the boat was moored at Cojímar, and it was here he met Gregorio Fuentes, who captained the *Pilar* until Hemingway left Cuba. The last time the pair used the boat was in a marlin competition in May 1960 – won by Fidel Castro. It is said that Fuentes was the inspiration for Santiago, the hero of *The Old Man and the Sea*, which won Hemingway the Nobel Prize in 1954. Fuentes was named a national hero by Fidel Castro in 1993, and regaled visitors with tales of Hemingway until he himself died in 2002 at the venerable age of 104.

The village is a pleasant place to stroll for a little while and watch the fishing boats out at sea. A bust of the author, made from brass boat fittings, looks out from the columned memorial beside the tiny, 17th-century La Chorrera fort.

To the east of Cojímar – follow the main coast road past the port – are the Playas del Este, a series of half a dozen beaches backed by resort hotels and popular on weekends with Habañeros (inhabitants of Havana) for whom the inviting beaches are within easy reach.

➕ 6B ✉ About 6 miles (10km) east of Havana 🍴 La Terraza ($$), ➤ 59

GUANABACOA

On the east side of Havana harbor, Guanabacoa is one of the city's oldest regions and served as the slave-trading center in colonial days. Calle Amargura – Bitterness Street – is so-called because slaves were marched along it. It also evolved as a major ecclesiastical center. Today much of the city is deteriorated, including its many churches and convents. An exception is the charming **Ermita de Potosí,** a tiny hermitage dating from 1644. The main interest is the **Museo Municipal,** in a fine colonial mansion, which has one of the best collections about Afro-Cuban cults on the island, including Santería and the minor cults of Regla de Palo (which originated in the Congo and has strong links with Haitian voodoo) and Abakuá (primarily a white Cuban cult and similar to the Freemasons). The Casa de Cultura is a center for preserving Cuba's African heritage, and there are frequent performances of traditional music and dance.

✚ *La Habana 8c (off map)*

Ermita de Potosí

✉ Calzada Vieja Guanabacoa esq Calle Potosí ☎ (07) 797-9867

🕐 Daily 8–5 ✋ Free

Museo Municipal

✉ Calle Martí 108 e/ San Antonio y Versalles ☎ (07) 797-9117

🕐 Daily 10–5 ✋ Inexpensive

HOTEL NACIONAL

One of Cuba's most famous hotels, the twin-towered Nacional has been visited by such diverse characters as Winston Churchill and Marlon Brando. In the 1950s it was the site of one of mobster Meyer Lansky's casinos. It fell on hard times, but was renovated in the early 1990s and is again one of the capital's most luxurious hotels. The downstairs bar has an interesting collection of photos of celebrities who have stayed there.

www.hotelnacionaldecuba.com

La Habana 3b ✉ Calle 21 esq O, Vedado ☎ (07) 873-3564

CASTILLO DE LOS TRES REYES DEL MORRO AND
FORTALEZA DE SAN CARLOS DE LA CABAÑA

Although the Cabaña fortress is the largest fort on the eastern side of Havana's harbor, it was not the first. That was El Morro, to the north, which was built over a 40-year period from 1589 with the twin objectives of protecting the harbour entrance and holding the high ground that dominated Havana. When the British attacked Cuba in 1762 they took El Morro and showed that control of the high ground was critical: Havana fell soon after. When the Spanish

regained Cuba they built Cabaña, arming the inland side of the fortress. This was the side from which the English had attacked as all its guns faced the sea. When completed in 1774 it was the largest fortress in the Americas and accommodated 5,000 soldiers.

Each fortress has a small museum, including one of Che Guevara's time as commander at Cabaña, and there is a lighthouse at El Morro with a great view. Cabaña is home to one of Cuba's most appealing traditions. At 9pm soldiers in 19th-century uniforms fire a cannon. In colonial times this told locals the city gates were about to close.

✚ *La Habana 8a and 7a* ✉ On the western side of Havana's harbor

El Morro

☎ (07) 863-7063 🕐 Daily 8–8 💰 Moderate

La Cabaña

☎ (07) 862-0617 🕐 Daily 10–10 💰 Moderate

MALECÓN

Best places to see, ➤ 44–45.

MUSEO DE ARTES DECORATIVAS

The Museum of Decorative Arts, housed in a palatial Vedado mansion built between 1924 and 1927, is brimful of colonial-era antiques (some 33,000 in all), recalling the days when it was occupied by the Countess Reveilla de Camargo, sister of the sugar baron José Gómez-Mena Vila. The furnishings are a showcase for the most opulent examples of the decorative arts. There are Italian marble-lined walls, mahogany doors, Venetian glass, Tiffany vases, Wedgwood china, Baccarat crystal, Meissen porcelain, 18th-century Chinese vases, furniture inlaid with mother-of-pearl and a marvelous art deco bathroom in stunning pink. In a mansion groaning with decorative wealth, the most outstanding of the rooms is the dining room, with its Aubusson tapestry-lined walls and table set with gold-trimmed crystalware. The society photographs lining the walls upstairs give a fascinating glimpse of the over-the-top lifestyle enjoyed by the cream of Havana society in the 1940s and 50s.

✚ *La Habana 1c* ✉ Calle 17, 502 e/ D y E ☎ (07) 832-0924 🕐 Tue–Sat 10–5 💰 Inexpensive

MUSEO HEMINGWAY

A little way south of Guanabacoa, in the hilltop village of San Francisco de Paula, is La Finca Vigía (Look-out Farm, so named for the military observation post that once topped the hill). The single-story farmhouse, set in 22 acres

(9 hectares) of gardens, was Ernest Hemingway's home for 20 years; it was seized by the Cuban government after his death and is now the Museo Hemingway. The house is closed (to prevent theft), but visitors can still view the rooms through the windows (open on dry days, closed on damp ones to preserve the contents). You can see the room where Hemingway worked, sometimes standing in front of the typewriter, for six hours daily. At Finca Vigía he wrote *The Old Man and the Sea* and his most controversial book, *Across the River and into the Trees*. In the well-kept grounds is the *Pilar*, the boat the writer sailed from Cojímar (➤ 98).

✠ *La Habana 7f (off map)*
✉ San Francisco de Paula
☎ (07) 891-0809
🕓 Mon–Sat 10–5, Sun 10–1. Closed on rainy days
💷 Inexpensive

MUSEO NAPOLEÓNICO

Cuba is almost the last place you would expect to find a museum about Napoleon Bonaparte, but this one, just behind the university in Vedado, is outstanding. The collection – which comprises more than 7,000 items – was acquired by a rich Habañero, Julio Lobo, whose fortune derived from Cuba's booming sugar trade years. You can see the hat Napoleon wore during his exile on St Helena and a pair of pistols he carried at Borodino, and a bronze death mask made by the former emperor's last doctor, Corsican Francesco Antommarchi, who retired to Cuba and died in Santiago. Antommarchi also supposedly brought body parts of Napoleon with him when he arrived in 1837, but their current whereabouts are unknown.

The museum occupies a restored Florentine mansion, originally built in 1928 by Orestes Ferrara, a Neapolitan who fought for the Cubans in the 1898 Spanish-American War. He later became a lawyer and then a politician and Cuban ambassador to France. Rooms have been sumptuously restored and furnished with statues, vases, paintings and objets d'art. The library is on the top floor; on the ground floor is a vast hall lit by

enormous decorated windows. At the back of the house is a small garden shaded by trees.

🕂 *La Habana 3c* ✉ Calle San Miguel 1159 esq Ronda ☎ (07) 879-1460 🕓 Tue–Sat 9:30–5, Sun 9:30–12:30 ✋ Inexpensive

PABELLÓN PARA LA MAQUETA DE LA CAPITAL

This modern pavilion contains a model of Havana, all 55 square miles (142sq km) of it, on a scale of 1:1,000. It took more than 10 years to build, and is an intriguing concept, allowing a better understanding of the development of the city. At the other end of the road, away from the sea, a left turn leads to a delightful park shaded by huge banyan trees.

🕂 *La Habana 1a (off map)* ✉ Calle 28, No 113 e/ 1 y 3 🕓 Mon–Sat 9:30–5 ✋ Inexpensive

PLAZA DE LA REVOLUCIÓN

The Plaza is used for national rallies, at which Raúl Castro addresses the crowd. It is also home to a towering obelisk, a monument to José Martí. At its base is a white marble statue of Martí, itself large, but completely dwarfed by the obelisk. Until the opening of the small but impressive **Memorial José Martí** at the base of the obelisk, guards would usher away

anyone careless enough to get too close to the statue and monument. Inside, you can take the lift to the lookout platform at the top and a stupendous view of the city. Behind the obelisk is the government headquarters building, including Castro's office. On the square's northern side the Ministry of the Interior building bears a vast outline rendering of the famous portrait of Che Guevara, complete with the Revolutionary slogan *"Hasta la Victoria Siempre"* (Ever Onward to Victory). Next door, the Ministry of Communications building has a Postal Museum, which will be of interest to philatelists, and a new metal outline rendering the portrait of Camilo Cienfuegos, one of the three rebel leaders of the 1959 Revolution.

✚ *La Habana 2e*

Memorial José Martí

☎ (07) 859-2347 ⊕ Mon–Sat 9–5 💷 Inexpensive

TROPICANA

The world-famous Tropicana cabaret is close to the Ciudad Libertad school complex (a former military airfield), some way from the center of Havana. Here, in past days, Maurice Chevalier, Carmen Miranda and Nat "King" Cole appeared, among others. It has been operating more or less continuously since its first night in 1931, and the show has changed little, the long-legged, scantily clad *mulata* girls being a clear link with another age. The show is performed beneath the stars and is great fun.

www.cabaret-tropicana.com

🕇 *La Habana 1a (off map)* ✉ Calle 72 e/ 41 y 45 ☎ (07) 267-1010
🕐 Tue–Sun, doors open at 8pm, show begins at 10pm 💷 Expensive

UNIVERSIDAD DE LA HABANA

Close to the Hotel Habana Libre is the campus of the University of Havana, founded by monks in 1728. A peaceful place after the hectic streets of Havana, there are two small, but interesting, museums. The Natural History Museum is Cuba's oldest museum, while the Montané Anthropological Museum has a fine collection of pre-Columbian artefacts.

www.uh.cu

🕇 *La Habana 2c* ✉ Calle San Lázaro y L ☎ (07) 878-3231
🕐 Museums: Mon–Fri 9–noon, 1–4 💷 Inexpensive 🍴 La Casona de 17 ($$$), ➤ 113

a drive southward from Havana

*Head eastward along the Malecón (▶ 44–45), going
through the tunnel that links the eastern and western
sides of Havana's harbor. You will pass the fortresses of
El Morro and La Cabaña (▶ 102–103). Continue along
the the Vía Monumental and then head clockwise along
the main highway. You will come to the Autopista
Nacional (A1) 12.5 miles (20km) into your journey. To
access the A1, look for a blue sign marked San Miguel,
indicated to the right. Directly after this sign, cross over
the A1 bridge and take the first signed exit to the right
onto the A1. After 1.2 miles (2km) traveling east on the
A1, a sign to the right signals Santa María del Rosario.*

The church in Santa María del Rosario is a fine colonial
church, with a beautiful gilt baroque altar and some lovely
late 18th-century murals (open Tue–Sat 8:30–11:30).

*Return to the highway (circunvalación) and continue
west for 9 miles (15km). There are no directional signs at
all, but just before the small blue 16th km road marker
there is a thatched roadside restaurant on the left.
Indicate to turn left off the highway. Cross right over the
intersection and into Parque Lenin (you will see a large
billboard advertising Parque Lenin but no road signs).*

Parque Lenin has hundreds of hectares of tree-scattered
parkland around a lake with a swimming pool, a horseback
riding center and steam train rides.

*Continue along Cortina de la Presa to reach its
intersection with Carretera del Rocio. Turn right for
1 mile (1.5km) to reach the **Jardin Botánico Nacional**
(National Botanical Garden).*

Although suffering a little from neglect, the garden is still a fine place, especially for its collection of native trees and shrubs, and the lovely Japanese collection.

> Reverse the route back to the main highway. Turn left on the highway until it reaches its intersection with Avenida de la Independencia (traffic lights). Turn right and follow the main road to Plaza de la Revolución. Bear right at the Y-junction just before the Plaza, then turn left at the major interchange beside the Castillo del Principe. Follow the road (Avenida de los Presidentes) to the Malecón.

Distance 50 miles (80km)
Time 5 hours including stops
Start/end point Malecón, Havana ✚ *La Habana 1a*
Lunch Las Ruinas ($$, ➤ 59), Cortina de la Presa, Parque Lenin; tel: (07) 644-2721
Jardin Botánico Nacional
✉ Carretera del Rocio ☎ (07) 697-9364 ⏱ Daily 9–4
✋ Inexpensive

HOTELS

Casa Particular de Jorge ($)
A delightful *casa particular* (licensed room rental) ideally situated close to the university and Malecón, in the heart of Vedado. The hosts are delightful, and the accommodation is comfy and clean.
✉ Calle I, No 456 e/ 21 y 23, Havana-Vedado ☎ (07) 832-9032; www.havanaroomrental.com

Conde de Villanueva ($$$)
Nine rooms surround a courtyard Valencia-style in this charming colonial mansion.
✉ Mercaderes 202 e/ Lamparilla y Amargura, Old Havana ☎ (07) 862-9293

Hotel Ambos Mundos ($$$)
See page 86–87.

Hotel Nacional ($$$)
See page 101.

Hotel Raquel ($$–$$$)
An elaborate centenary building converted into a stylish mid-priced hotel, with delightful furnishings and a wide range of services. Art deco flourishes throughout.
✉ San Ignacio esq Amargura, Old Havana ☎ (07) 860-8280

Hotel Saratoga ($$$)
Havana's (and Cuba's) most luxurious hotel, this sophisticated option is superbly located. Cosmopolitan decor, excellent service and a splendid bar and restaurant, all at a very high price.
✉ Prado 603, esq Dragones, Old Havana ☎ (07) 868-1000

Inglaterra ($$)
One of the oldest hotels in the capital, and one of the most distinctive buildings. Situated on Parque Central, with a pleasant atmosphere. Excellent piano bar. Mediocre rooms.
✉ Paseo de Martí (Prado) 416 esq Calle San Rafael, Havana-Vedado
☎ (07) 860-8594

Meliá Cohiba ($$$)

A luxury hotel in a splendid position near the Malecón. Well-appointed, but the North American/European standards come at a price.

✉ Avenida Paseo e/ 1 y 3, Havana-Vedado ☎ (07) 833-3636

Santa Isabel ($$$)

One of the most prestigious hotels in Havana, the Santa Isabel is housed in the *palacio* of Count Santovenia, and has a good restaurant, cafe, and rooftop bar.

✉ Plaza de Armas, Old Havana ☎ (07) 860-8201

Tryp Habana Libre ($$$)

Central, high-rise hotel with stylish atrium and great nighttime views. Excellent facilities, especially for business travelers, although rooms – and plumbing – are a let-down.

✉ Calle L e/ 23 y 25, Havana-Vedado ☎ (07) 838-4011

Valencia ($)

Small hotel in an 18th-century colonial mansion. A good restaurant specializing in paella. Reservations recommended.

✉ Calle Oficios 53 e/ Lamparilla y Obrapía, Old Havana ☎ (07) 867-1037

RESTAURANTS

El Aljibe ($$)

See page 58.

La Bodeguita del Medio ($$)

See page 77.

La Casona de 17 ($$$)

In an elegant mansion, the restaurant has a terrace with bar and grill serving inexpensive (but good) pizzas and chicken, and an indoor restaurant serving a better, more expensive, menu with some traditional Cuban meals.

✉ Calle 17, No 60 e/ N y M, Havana-Vedado ☎ (07) 838-3136 ⊕ Daily noon–midnight

El Floridita (00 000)

Bar beloved of Hemingway, but it is doubtful whether he would pay today's prices for "my daiquiri in the Floridita", or the seafood dishes. However, the history and ambience are entirely unique.

✉ Calle Obispo 557 esq Avenida de Bélgica, Habana Centro ☎ (07) 866-8856 🕐 Daily 12–11

La Guarida ($$$)

Havana's foremost *paladar* (private restaurant) draws the foreign elite with its bistro ambience and creative nouvelle dishes.

✉ Concordia e/ Gervaiso y Escobar, Habana Centro ☎ (07) 866-9047; www.laguarida.com 🕐 Daily noon–midnight

La Mina ($–$$)

Cuban food on an elegant garden patio with an enviable setting.

✉ Plaza de Armas, Old Havana ☎ (07) 862-0216 🕐 Daily noon–midnight

El Patio ($$$)

Housed in a fine mid-18th-century *palacio* adjacent to the cathedral. Unimpressive food, but worth a drink for the ambience.

✉ Plaza de la Catedral, Old Havana ☎ (07) 867-1035 🕐 Daily noon–midnight

Restaurante Santo Angel ($$$)

Delightful indoor and outdoor dining in a restored colonial mansion. Unusually creative dishes and live music while you dine.

✉ Plaza Vieja, Old Havana ☎ (07) 861-1626 🕐 Daily 11:30–11

Las Ruinas ($$)

An old sugar mill has been refurbished in very modern style. The menu is a mix of the expensive (lobster) and the inexpensive (Cuban dishes and pasta/pizza), but everything is well cooked.

✉ Cortina de la Presa, Parque Lenin ☎ (07) 644-2721 🕐 Tue–Fri noon–8, Sat, Sun 10–10

La Terraza de Cojímar ($$)

See page 59.

SHOPPING

Casa de l'Abanico

This new shop in Old Havana is entirely dedicated to fans. These must-have accessories in Cuba's humid climate range from plain colorful to intricately hand-painted and adorned with attachments. Your newly bought fan can be personalized by a painter in house for CUC0.50–5.

✉ Calle Obrapía 107 e/ Mercaderes y Oficios, Old Havana ☎ (07) 863-4452
🕐 Mon–Sat 10–7, Sun 10–1

Casa del Habano

Perhaps the best-stocked cigar store in Havana, with a vast range of labels and a separate VIP smoker's lounge (► 85).

✉ Fábrica de Tabacos Partagás, Calle Industria 524 e/ Barcelona y Dragones, Old Havana ☎ (07) 862-4604 🕐 Mon–Fri 9–7, Sat 9–5, Sun 10–4

Fería de la Artesanía

The largest artisans' market in Cuba, with a vast range of quality crafts. The best buys include lace womenswear, papier-mâché figurines, wooden sculptures and paintings.

✉ Almacenes San José, Old Havana 🕐 Daily 8:30–7

ENTERTAINMENT

Cabaret Parisien

Hot enough to cook the pork, this is Havana's second largest cabaret after Tropicana – with the same over-the-top costumes and heady mix of music – and sells out almost nightly.

✉ Hotel Nacional, Calle O, Havana-Vedado ☎ (07) 863-3663

Café Cantante Mi Habana

See page 62.

Casa de la Música

See page 62.

Clave y Guaguanco

See page 62.

Gato Tuerto

Cramped 1950s nightclub steeped in atmosphere. Tremendous performances, ranging from *bolero* to rap.

✉ Calle O e/ 17 y 19, Vedado ☎ (07) 838-2696

Habana Café

This distinctive nightclub combines a small cabaret, live music, and disco. The 1950s decor includes American classic autos and even an aircraft slung from the ceiling.

✉ Hotel Meliá Cohiba, Havana-Vedado ☎ (07) 833-3636 ext. 147

Macumba Habana

Favored by Havana's monied crowd (foreign businessfolk, Cuban models, the children of Communist bigwigs), this open-air cabaret-disco in the southwest suburbs is one of the hottest things in town.

✉ Centro Turístico La Giraldilla, Calle 222 e/ 37 y 51 ☎ (07) 273-0568

Palacio de la Salsa

A favorite of local salsa aficionados. A spicy cabaret warms things up, and live bands often perform.

✉ Hotel Riviera, Avenida Paseo esq Malecón, Havana-Vedado
☎ (07) 836-4051

Salón Turquino

Atop the Tryp Habana Libre hotel, this sizzling nightclub is one of the city's hottest dance spots. Live music and a tremendous nighttime vista of Havana.

✉ Tryp Habana Libre hotel, Calle 25 esq L, Havana-Vedado ☎ (07) 834-6100

Tropicana

See page 109.

La Zorra y el Cuervo

Premier subterranean jazz club packs in the crowds to hear such maestros as Chucho Váldes.

✉ Calle 23 e/ N y O, Havana-Vedado ☎ (07) 833-2402

Matanzas and Western Cuba

The western third of the island is a region of dramatic contrast, with some of the most quintessential of all Cuban landscapes.

Península de Zapata (➤ 50) is the largest wetland in the entire Caribbean. Here there are species not only unique to Cuba, but endemic to the swampland, a pristine habitat of vital importance. Zapata can be reached on a day trip from Varadero, Cuba's foremost beach resort, where large-scale modern hotels line the white sands of the Atlantic shore. Nearby is Matanzas, a historically significant trade center with important buildings and caves to explore, plus one of Cuba's most scintillating cabarets.

To the west, the long tapering peninsula of Pinar del Río is renowned for its *mogotes* (dramatic limestone formations) and for its fertile tobacco fields. Scuba diving is first-class off the north and far western shores, as it is to the south of Isla de la Juventud, a large island slung beneath the belly of Havana province. The isle has Cuba's foremost dive site, while the tiny coral cays sprinkled across the turquoise seas further east culminate in Cayo Largo, with perhaps the finest beaches in all of Cuba.

Matanzas

MATANZAS

Originally sandwiched between two rivers, the Yumurí and the San Juan, Matanzas has now grown into a sizeable industrial city and port. After its foundation in the latter part of the 17th century, the city quickly became a major port for reprovisioning ships en route to Spain.

The city's name, which derives from "slaughter", may be a reminder of the herds of animals brought to the town, slaughtered and loaded on to the ships. Matanzas was also an important sugar port, and a slave-trading center. It has since evolved a rich Afro-Cuban culture, is important as a nexus of Santería, and is second only to Santiago de Cuba as a birthplace of traditional culture. The town is backed by a mountain called "Sleeping Beauty" by the locals as it is thought to look like a reclining pregnant woman. The drive along the coast toward Havana is one of the best on Cuba, with great views of the Yumurí valley, particularly at Bayacunyagua, where vultures soar on the thermals.

Today Matanzas is a slightly faded place, but its old center is still worth visiting. Yet here, just a short distance from the tourist enclave of Varadero, is the real Cuba.

✚ 8C

Castillito de San Severino

Built in 1745 to guard the entrance to Matanzas harbor, this small yet sturdy fortress has been partially restored, with cannon in situ. It houses the Museo de la Ruta de Esclavo, tracing the history and impact of slavery, as well as an excellent exhibition about Afro-Cuban religions, highlighted by life-size gods, or *orishas*. The moat once doubled as an execution ground, and bulletholes can be seen in the walls.

✉ 0.25 miles (400m) east of Avenida 230, northeast of downtown ☎ (045) 28-3259 🕐 Mon–Sat 9–5, Sun 9–1 🖑 Inexpensive

Catedral de San Carlos Borromeo

It is odd to find a Spanish cathedral in Cuba dedicated to an Italian saint. The 16th-century Cardinal Archbishop of Milan was, locals said, too ugly to be anything but a saint, but he was a tireless worker for Christianity. The late 19th-century building is on the site of a much earlier one destroyed by fire. Though in need of a good cleaning, the cathedral is still an impressive sight. Inside, the frescoed walls and ceilings are a delight.

✉ Calle 83 esq 282 🕐 Mon–Fri 8–noon, 3–5; Sun 9–noon 🍴 Café Atenas ($), Calle 83 esq 272

Cuevas de Bellamar

A regular destination from Varadero, the Bellamar caves extend for about 1.6 miles (2.5km) – though only about 2,460ft/750m are open to the public – and have some beautiful rock formations. The 85ft-high (26m) cavern has a stream and unique crystal formations.

✉ Finca La Alcancia, 6km (4 miles) southeast of Matanzas ☎ (045) 25-3538

🕐 Tue–Sun 9:30–5 (tours, lasting about 45 mins, start about every hour)

✋ Moderate 🍴 There is a small cafe on site ($) 🚌 Join an organized tour from Varadero

Museo Farmacéutico
Situated on the southern side of the Plaza de la Libertad, just a little way west of the cathedral, the Pharmaceutical Museum is housed in a pharmacy opened by a Frenchman in 1822. Almost all the jars and dishes, bottles, tools and recipes for producing all manner of ointments and potions have been preserved – absolutely fascinating.

✉ Plaza de la Libertad ☎ (045) 24-3179 ⏰ Mon–Sat 10–5, Sun 10–2
💵 Inexpensive 🍴 Café Atenas ($), Calle 83 esq 272

Palacio Junco
Close to the bay, this fine late 19th-century house of a plantation owner is now a museum to Matanzas' history. The museum includes a good section on slavery and the local sugar industry.

✉ Plaza de la Vigía ☎ (045) 24-3464 ⏰ Tue–Fri 10–6, Sat–Sun 9–noon
💵 Inexpensive 🍴 Café Atenas ($), Calle 83 esq 272

Plaza de la Vigía
The San Juan river is crossed by the Puente Calixto García, a movable steel structure erected in the 19th century. On its town side the bridge ends in this delightful square, where, on 1 January 1899, after the city had been bombarded by the U.S. battleship *New York*, the Spanish surrendered to General Sanger of the U.S. army. On the southern edge of the square the town fire brigade still occupies a fine neoclassical building dating from 1897. Inside there are several antique fire engines. Opposite the station is a gallery showing work by local artists.

🍴 Cafe Atenas ($)

Teatro Sauto

Across the road from the fire station is the town theater, built by public subscription in the mid-19th century and one of the finest neo-classical buildings on the island. In its heyday it was the scene of glittering shows by some great artists, including Caruso and Anna Pavlova, and it still has regular events. If you are unable to catch a show, ask for a tour: it is worthwhile for the glorious paintings of the Muses on the ceiling.

✉ Plaza de la Vigía ☎ (045) 24-2721 🕐 Daily 9–5 💵 Inexpensive

Western Cuba

BAHÍA DE COCHINOS

Castro's nationalization agenda, and the forging of trade links with the communist world after the revolution, brought US antagonism towards Castro to boiling point. Finally, in April 1961, a force of US-trained anti-Castro Cuban émigrés came ashore at the Bay of Pigs. The Cuban Air Force attacked the invasion force's support ships, forcing them to withdraw, as President Kennedy would not countenance direct intervention. Within three days, after several hundred on both sides had been killed, the beleaguered invasion force surrendered. Castro found himself with more than 1,000 prisoners that he was later able to trade for supplies.

The Cubans named the invasion for the Bay's beach, Playa Girón. A small yet excellent museum, **Museo de Girón,** in the village has a collection mainly of photographs and documents, but also weapons, Soviet and American tanks and a British-made Sea Fury fighter flown by the Cuban Air Force.

Most visitors come in search of the invasion, and many miss the bay itself. The crystal-clear sea is ideal for diving and swimming – the whole eastern shore from Playa Larga to Playa Girón is a delight. The inlet is also famous for its sea life, including (in May and June) thousands of crabs that heedlessly cross the road (especially at dawn and dusk) during mating season, causing a puncture hazard when drivers run over them.

At Cueva de los Peces you can rent flippers and snorkels to swim in an 260ft-deep (80m) submerged cave among jewel-like shoals of tropical fish.

✚ 9D 🚌 Taxi from Jagüey Grande to Playa Girón

Museo de Girón

✉ Playa Girón 📞 (045) 98-4122 🕐 Daily 8–5 ✋ Inexpensive 🍴 Caleta Buena ($$), Playa Girón, serves drinks and food next to natural pools for snorkeling

CÁRDENAS

Situated about 12 miles (20km) from Varadero, Cárdenas is a fine city, though in need of significant refurbishment. The city was not founded until 1828, which gives its center a pleasing architectural wholeness. At the city's heart is the cathedral, most notable for the quality of its stained glass. The cathedral stands on the northern edge of Parque Colón, named for the statue of Christopher Columbus, which was sculpted in 1862, making it the oldest statue of the great explorer in the Americas.

From the cathedral, head south along Avenida Céspedes to reach Calle 12; turn left to reach two good museums. The first is **Casa Natal de José Antonio Echevarría**, where the student leader was born in 1932. Shot dead at the entrance of Havana

University in 1957, he has become a national hero, and the museum has memorabilia about him, as well as a general historical collection.

Close to the Echevarría museum is the **Museo Oscar María de Rojas** – perhaps the finest museum outside Havana – with an eclectic collection including butterflies, minerals, Amerindian objects, photographs, coins, weapons and an extraordinary 19th-century hearse.

A right turn at Calle 12 leads to Plaza Malakoff, the city's old market square. The Market Hall, built in the 1840s, is a remarkable two-storey iron construction in the shape of a cross with an iron dome 52.5ft (16m) high.

✚ 9C

🍴 Café Esprun ($), Calle 12 e/ Avenida 4 y 6

Casa Natal José Antonio Echevarría
✉ Calle 12 esq Avenida 4
☎ (045) 52-4145
🕐 Tue–Sat 10–6, Sun 9–1 ✋ Inexpensive

Museo Oscar María de Rojas
✉ Calle 12 e/ Avenida 4 y 6 ☎ (045) 52-2417
🕐 Tue–Sat 9–6, Sun 9–1
✋ Moderate

125

CAYO LARGO

Around 1,600 islands and cays (shallow reef islands, from the Spanish *cayo*) surround Cuba. Cayo Largo – one of the prettiest of them all – lies south of the Zapata Peninsula, in the same archipelago (the Canarreos) as Cuba's largest island, Isla de la Juventud (➤ 130–131). It is about 17 miles (27km) long and 3 miles (5km) wide at its widest point, and is the island paradise of dreams – white sand surrounded by a clear, turquoise sea. Cayo Largo was a haunt of pirates in the 17th and 18th centuries, but until the early 1980s it had never been inhabited on a full-time basis. The government has since developed it as a resort island with several state-owned, all-inclusive hotels. Most visitors are package tourists, but day or overnight trips are also available by air from Havana and Varadero.

Virtually the whole of the island's southern shore is beach, with the advantage of clean sand and warm water. Water sports are popular, as is wreck diving – the island's reefs have ensnared several ships in the past. Swimming can be dangerous because of an undertow and odd currents: watch for the red flags on the beaches. The eastern end of the island, the aptly named Playa Tortuga, is a nesting ground for sea turtles. Turtles can also be seen at a conservation hatchery at Combinado, the island's only settlement (for workers), where a small fishing lodge is located. From Combinado, boat trips are available to Cayo Iguana, a small island off Largo's western tip. The iguanas of the name are numerous and tame, but they are on Cayo Largo too. Cayo Rosario, an uninhabited island, can also be visited.

✚ 8E ✉ 37 miles (60km) south of Zapata Peninsula ✖ Regular flights from Havana and Varadero

GUAMÁ AND LAGUNA DEL TESORO

The wildest parts of the Zapata Peninsula have already been described (➤ 50–51), but for the less intrepid there is much else to see on the peninsula. The Bay of Pigs and the beaches on its eastern shore (➤ 122–123) are the most obvious attraction, but Guamá and Laguna del Tesoro (Treasure Lake) are also worth visiting. Hotel Guamá was one of Fidel Castro's first ventures into tourism. Built across a dozen or so bridge-linked artificial islands in Treasure Lake, Guamá is a purpose-built tourist village with wooden huts in the style of Cuba's Amerindians.

At Boca de Guamá is the **Criadero de Crocodrilos,** where the native Cuban crocodile is bred. The project is in part a conservation exercise for the once-endangered species, but also supplies skins for the various handicrafts on sale, and meat for the nearby restaurant. If you are tempted to buy, you must obtain a certificate from the shop or Cuban (and international) customs may confiscate the purchase: wild crocodiles are protected and poaching, though rare, does occur. Fascinating tours of the *criadero* are offered, as are fishing tours in the lake.

From the village, boats take you through a canal to the main lake (Laguna del Tesoro) to visit Villa Guamá. The lake is so called because of a legend that the local Amerindians, after bravely resisting the Spanish, threw their most treasured possessions into the lake rather than have them fall into Spanish hands. Their leader was called Guamá. Around the village are a number of wooden sculptures of Amerindians in a supposed reconstruction of native village life, designed by Cuba's most famous sculptor, Rita Longa.

➕ 9D 🍴 Hotel Guamá ($) ☎ (045) 91-9100 🚌 Taxis from Jagüey Grande to Playa Girón; also GuamáBusTour buses run twice a day from Boca de Guamá to Playa Girón

Criadero de Crocodrilos

✉ Boca de Guamá ☎ (045) 91-5562 🕐 Daily 8–6 💵 Moderate
🍴 El Colibrí ($$), Boca de Guamá

ISLA DE LA JUVENTUD

Lying about 56 miles (90km) off the mainland's southern coast, Isla de la Juventud, the Island of Youth, is the largest of Cuba's offshore islands. The almost circular island is about 25 miles (40km) across. It was once favored by pirates and reputedly called *Treasure Island*. There are many who believe Robert Louis Stevenson's Treasure Island was based on it: Stevenson never came here, but the topography of the real and fictional islands is intriguingly similar. It was named Island of Youth in 1978, when Cuba gave free education to thousands of young Africans here. Most of the island's population live on the north side; the southern shore – an almost continuous stretch of white sand with some of the world's best diving sites – is cut off by the huge Lanier marsh, which is still home to Cuban crocodiles (and large numbers of fearsome mosquitoes).

Nueva Gerona, the island's capital, with its rows of wooden houses, has several paltry museums (the best is the **Natural History Museum**), a fine

church and the hulk of the boat *El Pinero*, now beached as a memorial, which once ferried Fidel Castro to liberty. To the south of the town, the **Museo Finca El Abra** is where José Martí stayed during his imprisonment here.

The four five-story, circular buildings of the **Presidio Modelo** used to house several thousand prisoners. It was here that Fidel Castro and the other prisoners of the Moncada attack (➤ 168) were brought. The prison is now, in part, a museum of that episode.

The Caribbean's most important set of Amerindian pictographs are to be found in caves close to Punta del Este. There are over 200 in all, dating from as early as 1000BC through to AD800. An official guide is required to visit the south of the isle.

➕ 5E ✖ By plane from Havana, several flights daily 🚢 Hydrofoil or ferry from Surgidero de Batabanó four times daily

Museo de Ciencias Naturales/Planetario

✉ Calle 41 esq 46, Nueva Gerona ☎ (046) 32-3143 🕐 Tue–Sat 9am–10pm, Sun 9–1 ♿ Inexpensive 🍴 Restaurante Dragon ($), Calle 39, near the church

Museo Finca El Abra

✉ 2 miles (3km) southwest of Nueva Gerona ☎ (05) 219-3054 (cell phone) 🕐 Tue–Sat 9–4, Sun 9–1 ♿ Inexpensive

Presidio Modelo

✉ 2.5 miles (4km) east of Nueva Gerona ☎ (046) 32-5112 🕐 Mon–Sat 8–4, Sun 8–noon ♿ Inexpensive

PENÍNSULA DE GUANAHACABIBES

At the extreme west of Pinar del Río there are more fine beaches in the Bahía Corrientes. To the north, a freshwater lake – Laguna Grande – is famous for its fishing. Bahía Corrientes is excellent for diving, the local center being at María la Gorda. Whale sharks are often seen in the bay, which features spectacular coral walks, caves and even Spanish galleons.

Beyond the bay the road enters the Guanahacabibes National Park, a UNESCO-backed biosphere reserve on the far western peninsula of Cuba. It was here that Cuba's Arawak Indians made their last stand against the Spanish invaders. Within the reserve wild pigs still roam on the low-lying limestone. The area is also important as a feeding stop for migrating birds, particularly in the winter months, and as a breeding ground for turtles. Diving and fishing are available at Playa Las Tumbas.

⊞ 1E–2D 🚌 By taxi or tour bus only, no buses

PENÍNSULA DE VARADERO

On the north coast, about 90 miles (145km) east of Havana, Varadero – the tourist capital of Cuba – occupies a long, narrow peninsula that extends into the Atlantic Ocean. Around the turn of the 20th century, rich Habañeros built second homes along the shore. Then, in 1926, Irénee Du Pont (of the French-American chemical giant) bought most of the land, built himself a home and persuaded other rich Americans to join him. Du Pont's home – Xanadú – is now the Las Américas restaurant and a small hotel, with a spectacular position above crashing waves. The Varadero golf course is also here.

After the revolution Varadero's fortunes fell, but they have been revived by the recent tourism boom. Two-thirds of all hotel rooms in Cuba are here: the majority are large-scale, all-inclusive resorts catering to package tourists seeking little more than sea, sand and sun. The resort is in the main a foreign tourist enclave, and visitors get virtually no sense of Cuban reality. Still, the sands are lovely and shelve into bathtub warm, jade-colored waters. Parque Josone is a peaceful landscaped park with a lake and cafes, and is a popular spot for *quinceñeras* (girls celebrating their 15th birthday) to have their photographs taken. Elsewhere on the isthmus, the Cueva de Ambrosia is decorated with important pre-Columbian pictographs, and trails lead through the dry forests of Varahicacos Ecological Reserve, virtually the only undeveloped part of the peninsula. Dolphins perform tricks at the Delfinario, and you can swim with these marine mammals for a hefty fee. Diving, snorekling and catamaran safaris are a popular option for day trips.

✚ 9B ✉ Off the Vía Blanca highway 🍴 Las Américas ($$–$$$; ➤ 58)
🚌 Regular buses to Varadero from Havana and Matanzas
ℹ Infotur, Calle 13 y Avenida 1; tel: (04) 66-2691

PENÍNSULA DE ZAPATA

Best places to see, ➤ 50–51.

a walk around Pinar del Río

With your back to the Teatro Milanes, head west (left) toward Plaza de la Independencia, and then take the first left along Calle Isabel Rubio. Follow the road across three crossroads and continue on to the Casa Garay liqueur factory, on your left.

Pinar is famous for the production of *guayabita*, a potent liqueur made by adding rum to *guayabita* fruit – a small, wild version of the guava, looking much like a rose hip – mixed with water and sugar. The concoction is left to steep for 30 days and then barrelled for a couple of months. The factory **(Fábrica de Bebidas Casa Garay)** is now the only place in town where it is made, and it produces 300 bottles a day. A shop at the factory sells the liqueur, which comes in two forms: Guayabita Liqueur is amazingly sweet, while Guayabita Seca is mouth-puckeringly dry. The Seca is more alcoholic, but local wisdom has it that each is made more palatable by adding water.

Retrace your steps from the factory, take the first left turn and walk down Calle Cefarino Fernández to Calle Gerardo Medina. Turn right here to reach the Catedral de San Rosendo.

The neoclassical, peach melba-colored cathedral with its two bell towers was built in the late 19th century; it's only open in the afternoon.

Turn left along Calle Antonio Maceo, crossing Calle Ormoni Arenado, to pass the birthplace of Antonio Guiteras Holmes at No 52.

Holmes, a 1930s revolutionary, was executed in 1935 near Matanzas.

Cross Calle Rafael Morales and continue toward Plaza de la Independencia. The cigar factory (➤ 135) is to the left. Within the square there is an interesting shop selling local arts and crafts. Bear right across the square and turn right into Calle Martí, following it back to the theater.

Distance 1.5 miles (2.5 km)
Time 1.5 hours, plus at least 2 hours for sightseeing
Start/end point Teatro Milanés on Calle Martí
Lunch La Casona ($); ➤ 141
Fábrica de Bebidas Casa Garay
✉ Calle Isabel Rubio 189 ☎ (048) 75-2966 🕙 Mon–Fri 8–5
♿ Free

PINAR DEL RÍO

This once pretty town takes its name from the pines beside the Río Guamá. Pinar has always been a wealthy place, the local soil growing Cuba's best tobacco. Because of the town's economic importance, and the tourist potential of the nearby Viñales Valley (► 54–55), it was linked to Havana by an early *autopista*. Nonetheless, five decades of communism have taken a severe toll on the city.

Entering the town from the *autopista* – which becomes Calle Martí, the main street, with an array of excellent neo-classical houses – the first place of interest is Palacio Guasch (*c*1910), to the left. A colonial mansion with a curious mixture of decoration – Greek columns, gothic spires and gargoyles – it now houses the **Museo de Ciencias Naturales** (Natural History Museum). Further on, also to the left, is the **Museo Provincial de Historia** (Provincial Museum), with memorabilia of composer Pedro Junco and a sparse collection of glassware, furniture and, unusually, police truncheons. In the middle of the town, the restored Teatro Milanés was built entirely of wood in the early 19th century. At the far end of Calle Martí is the town's only remaining tobacco factory, **Fábrica de Tabacos.** Here visitors can watch the hand-rolling of cigars.

✚ 4D

Museo de Ciencias Naturales

✉ Calle Martí 202 ☎ (048) 77-9483 🕐 Mon–Sat 9–4:45, Sun 9–1
✋ Inexpensive 🍴 La Casona ($); ➤ 141

Museo Provincial de Historia

✉ Calle Martí 58
☎ (048) 75-4300
🕐 Tue–Sat 8am–10pm, Sun 9–1 ✋ Inexpensive

Fábrica de Tabacos

✉ Calle Máceo 157, Plaza de la Independencia
☎ (048) 77-2244
🕐 Mon–Fri 9–noon, 1–4, Sat–Sun 9–noon
✋ Moderate

VIÑALES

Best places to see, ➤ 54–55.

VUELTA ABAJO

West of Pinar del Río the land becomes increasingly marshy. This region, around San Juan y Martínez, is known as Vuelta Abajo, and is almost exclusively given over to tobacco growing. It produces the best tobacco on the island, and some plantations offer tours. Further west is the Bahía de Cortéz, a large and beautiful bay. There is little development here and beaches such as Playa Ballén are ideal for those seeking an entirely natural Cuba.

✚ 3D ✉ About 12 miles (20km) southwest of Pinar del Río

a drive through Western Cuba

This long but worthwhile drive will take a full day, although it is suggested that you overnight in Viñales (➤ 54–55). An early start is recommended.

From Havana, head south from Plaza de la Revolución to reach the start of the Havana–Pinar del Río autopista. Follow it toward Pinar. After about 56 miles (90km) leave the autopista at the exit for Soroa and drive to this exquisite town high in the Sierra del Rosario.

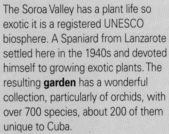

The Soroa Valley has a plant life so exotic it is a registered UNESCO biosphere. A Spaniard from Lanzarote settled here in the 1940s and devoted himself to growing exotic plants. The resulting **garden** has a wonderful collection, particularly of orchids, with over 700 species, about 200 of them unique to Cuba.

A rainbow often forms across the nearby waterfall, explaining why the Soroa Valley is sometimes called the Rainbow of Cuba. Keen swimmers can take a dip in the pool at the bottom of the falls.

Return to the autopista and continue to Pinar del Río (➤ 136–137). Here turn right just beyond Teatro Milanés (Calle Isabel Rubio/Carreteria Central), then left – opposite the gas station – for the Viñales Valley (➤ 54–55).

The quickest way back to Havana is to retrace the route along the *autopista*.

Alternatively, if time permits, follow the narrow, winding valley road that runs close to the north coast, a road with beautiful views of the sea through pine forests. Continue to Orlando Nodarse, then bear left for Mariel and the north coast autopista, *which leads to Miramar and on to the Malecón* (► 44–45).

Distance 217 miles (350km)

Time 12 hours, including stops

Start/end point Havana
✛ 6B

Lunch Casa de Don Tomás ($–$$; ► 143) serves *criolla* food

Soroa Orchid Garden
☎ (048) 52-3871
🕐 Daily 8:30–5. Guided tours half-hourly
✋ Inexpensive 🍽 Villa Soroa ($)

HOTELS

BAHÍA DE COCHINOS
Villa Playa Larga ($–$$)
Fairly basic, with rooms in concrete bungalows, but an ideal base for birdwatching and snorkeling. The restaurant is adequate. Water sports on offer.

✉ Playa Larga ☎ (045) 98-7294

CAYO LARGO
Sol Cayo Largo ($$$)
By far the best of the several all-inclusive resort hotels here, this one has spacious rooms behind the beach. Splendid facilities include a beachfront restaurant, water sports and entertainment.

✉ Cayo Largo ☎ (045) 24-8260

GUAMÁ
Hotel Guamá ($)
The ideal place from which to explore the beautiful Zapata Peninsula (➤ 50–51), but also close to the idyllic Bay of Pigs. Swimming pool and boating on the lake. Guests stay in Amerindian-style thatched cabins.

✉ At Treasure Lake, north of the Bay of Pigs

PINAR DEL RÍO
Hotel Vuelta Abajo ($$)
In a lovingly restored colonial-era hotel, this is the nicest place for miles. Modest but comfy accommodations, the best restaurant in town, plus a bar, internet cafe and pharmacy.

✉ Martí 103, esq. Rafael Morales ☎ (048) 75-9381

SIERRA DEL ROSARIO
Hotel La Moka ($$–$$$)
A remarkable development within the UNESCO biosphere reserve, reached by paths winding through the vegetation. Excellent Creole restaurant. Charming, air-conditioned rooms with full facilities.

✉ Las Terrazas ☎ (048) 57-8600

VARADERO

Hotel Varadero Internacional ($–$$)

The Internacional was the first hotel built on Varadero beach, and its fabulous marble 1950s entrance takes you straight back to that era. The rooms are spacious and comfortable though some need an upgrade, the staff are friendly, and it's right on the beach.

✉ Avenida Las Américas km1 ☎ (045) 66-7038; www.gran-caribe.com

Mansión Xanadú ($$$)

This hotel was formerly Irenée Du Pont's home (► 133). The six rooms retain their period furnishings. There's a superb restaurant (► 58), and golf and sand are just steps away.

✉ Avenida Las Américas ☎ (045) 66-8482

Riu Varadero ($$$)

Situated at the eastern end of the Varadero peninsula, this stylish new hotel has a pool, a spa and glorious stretch of beach.

✉ Autopista Sur km 18.5 ☎ (045) 66-7966

VIÑALES

La Ermita ($$)

On a hilltop with superb valley views. Fully air-conditioned rooms, excellent restaurant (Cuban and international menus) and swimming pool.

✉ About 1.2 miles (2km) east of Viñales ☎ (048) 79-6071

Los Jazmines ($$)

Stunning views of the Viñales valley. Explore the countryside (rent horses from the hotel) or relax by the pool. Air-conditioned.

✉ About 2.5 miles (4km) south of Viñales ☎ (048) 79-6205

RESTAURANTS

PINAR DEL RÍO

La Casona ($)

Opposite the Teatro Milanés in a pleasant colonial mansion. La Casona's menu includes Cuban-style dishes.

✉ Calle Martí esq Colón, Pinar del Río ☎ (048) 77-8263 ⊕ Daily 11:30–11:30

Rumayor ($$)

This thatch restaurant decorated in Polynesian style has a *criollo* menu with signature dishes such as *pollo ahumado,* smoked chicken, and *pollo Rumayor,* the house chicken grilled and served with a spicy sauce. Both cabaret and restaurant are open air, adding to the atmosphere.

✉ About 0.6 miles (1km) north of Pinar del Río on the road to Viñales
☎ (048) 76-3007 🕐 Daily noon–midnight

VARADERO

Las Américas ($$–$$$)

See page 58.

El Bodegón Criollo ($$)

Interesting decor, with the menu written up on a chalkboard. Specializes in Cuban dishes and does them rather well.

✉ Avenida de la Playa esq Calle 40 ☎ (045) 66-7784 🕐 Daily noon–11

Casa de Al ($$–$$$)

Dine right on the beach at Al Capone's holiday home. The blue-paint and stone house was used by the Mafia boss to store bootleg rum for liquor runs to Prohibition-era US. The small, intimate restaurant serves up a Mafia-themed menu of dishes like mafiosa soup and cold blood ice-cream.

✉ Avenida Kawama ☎ (045) 66-8018 🕐 Daily 10–10

Dante ($$$)

The most expensive place in town. Beautifully sited in the park and with an excellent international (mainly Italian) menu.

✉ Parque Josone ☎ (045) 66-7728 🕐 Daily noon–midnight

Restaurante El Fondue ($$$)

Specializing in fondues, this elegant restaurant also offers surprisingly varied and well-prepared steaks and seafood. One of the best restaurants outside the Varadero hotels.

✉ Avenida 1ra esq 62 ☎ (045) 66-7747 🕐 Daily noon–10

VINALES
Casa de Don Tomás ($–$$)
In a 19th-century replica wooden colonial mansion, this is a very friendly place selling fried chicken and other simple meals, plus a few surprises. *Las Delicás de Don Tomás* is a mix of seafood, pork and chicken, sausage of undefined heritage and rice all arranged around fried eggs.

✉ At the western end of Viñales ☎ (08) 79-6300 ⏰ Daily 10–10

ENTERTAINMENT

Cabaret Continental
Feast your eyes on the famous cabaret at the Hotel Internacional. You can also dine while watching the twirling dancers.

✉ Hotel Varadero Internacional, Avenida Las Américas, Varadero ☎ (045) 66-7038 ⏰ Thu–Sun dinner at 8pm, show 10pm

La Comparsita
Eclectic shows at this open-air venue include cabarets, magicians, and singers. A disco follows.

✉ Calle 60 esq. Avenida 3ra, Varadero ☎ (045) 66-7415

Cueva del Pirata
Small cabaret on a pirate theme in a perfect venue – a cave. Dancing afterward.

✉ On the Autopista Sur at the 6.8 miles (11km) point (just east of the Hotel Sol Palmeras), Varadero ☎ (045) 66-7751

Discoteca Las Cuevas
A large cavern full of stalagmites and stalactites forms a tremendous stage for a cabaret, then the chance to dance.

✉ 2.5 miles (4km) north of Viñales ☎ (048) 79-6290 ⏰ Sat only

Havana Club
Established and popular dance club playing a variety of music from world beat to hip-hop and salsa.

✉ Centro Comercial Copey, Avenida 3 esq Calle 62, Varadero ☎ (045) 61-4555

Mambo Club
The top nightspot in Varadero. Retro decor and tremendous disco ambience with occasional live music and cabaret.

✉ Avenida Las Américas, Varadero ☎ (045) 66-8565

Rumayor
This small Las Vegas-style cabaret followed by a disco is about the only night-scene in town, and the show goes on until 3am. Open-air.

✉ On the road towards Viñales, Pinar del Río ☎ (048) 76-3007

Tropicana Matanzas
Scintillating open-air, themed cabaret with high-kicking showgirls.

✉ Autopista Varadero km 4.5 ☎ (045) 26-5555

SPORT

Centro Internacional de Buceo Barracuda
This is the principal dive center in downtown Varadero, offering dives, courses, water sports and catamaran trips. The staff are very helpful.

✉ Calle 59 and Avenida 1ra, Varadero ☎ (045) 61-3481; www.nauticamarlin.com

Centro Internacional de Buceo Cólony
Good organized dives for experienced and novice divers.

✉ Hotel El Colony, Isla de la Juventud ☎ (046) 39-8181

Centro Internacional de Deportes Aéreos
See Cuba from around 10,000ft (3,000m) up. Skydiving is on offer from Varadero's old airport, with novice parachutists being strapped to an expert. The experience is costly (though you do get a free T-shirt and a certificate).

✉ The old airport to the west of Varadero ☎ (045) 66-7256

Dive Center Octopus
A variety of organized dives to suit all abilities are offered here.

✉ Playa Larga ☎ (045) 98-7284

Cienfuegos and Central Cuba

To the east of Varadero and the Zapata Peninsula lies the agricultural heart of Cuba. Here grows enough sugar to sweeten all the coffee cups in the world. This is also the land of the cattle ranch and the *vaquero,* the Cuban cowboy, while the tobacco fields of Santa Clara province are tended by *guajiros,* hardy, salt-of-the-earth Cuban farmers. Dressed in loose-fitting shirt and trousers and a de rigeur straw hat to keep off the sun, they still till the fields using ox-drawn plows, adding a lyrical note to the landscape.

In this part of Cuba, too, is Trinidad, the most famous and best-preserved colonial town on the island. Remedios, though less well known, is almost Trinidad's equal; Santa Clara, with its impressive monument and museum to Che Guevara, is where Che fought the battle that won the revolutionary war, while from the heights of the Escambray Mountains the view of the Caribbean is incomparable.

CIENFUEGOS

The Jagua Castle (▶ below) protected the
narrow entrance to Cienfuegos' vast
harbor from the mid-18th century, but the
town itself was not founded until 1819.
Louis Clouet, a Frenchman, persuaded the
Cuban Governor General to allocate land to
people from Louisiana, which the US had

just bought from France. Governor Cienfuegos agreed, and each
of the new settlers was given a parcel of land by the harbor.
In thanks, the settlers named their new town after him.

Soon Cienfuegos had become one of Cuba's major ports, its
wealth reflected in the rows of buildings at the heart of the city,
most of them in French neoclassical style. The huge natural
harbor – it was claimed at the end of the 19th century that all
the world's navies could safely anchor within its confines –
ensured the city's continuing prosperity. After the revolution the
Soviets moored submarines here, and poured in money to
develop industries at the harbor fringe. Among other things,
Cienfuegos boasts Cuba's biggest cement works and, to the
southwest at Juraguá, its only nuclear power plant. Construction
here began in 1980, but with the fall of the Soviet empire work
stopped in 1992. The city's industrial power base, however, is
set for expansion. The Chinese are to invest US$6 billion in its oil
refinery, co-owned by the Cuban government and Venezuela's
state-owned Petroleos de Venezuela.

✚ 10D

Castillo de Jagua

The Castillo de Nuestra Señora de los Ángeles de Jagua (Castle
of Our Lady of the Angels of Jagua) stands on the western
approach to Cienfuegos' harbor. It was built in the 1740s, a time
when the island had a thriving business relationship with pirates
and privateers, and was under threat from the British. The castle

is said to be haunted by a lady in blue, reputedly the wife of a former governor of the castle. One night, the story goes, a soldier attacked the ghost. Dawn found him completely insane, with blue cloth wrapped around his sword. The lady was never seen again.

✉ At the western approach to Cienfuegos' harbor 🕐 Mon–Sat 9:30–5, Sun 9:30–1 ✋ Inexpensive

Palacio del Valle

The exotic Palacio del Valle, at the southern edge of the city, is said to have been built by Moroccans at the request of a local industrialist, which explains the Moorish (though not the Gothic) touches. Today it houses a very good restaurant (➤ 58).

✉ At the southern end of Calle 37 (Paseo del Prado), beside the Hotel Jagua ☎ (043) 55-1003 🕐 Daily noon–10 ✋ Inexpensive 🍴 Restaurant ($–$$$) in palace

Parque José Martí

Any visit to Cienfuegos must start at Parque José Martí, the neat and shady square at the center of the old town. On the park's eastern edge is the Catedral de la Purisima Concepción, a plain but dignified twin-towered building. Its treasure is a series of 12 windows, depicting the Apostles in French stained glass. On the square's northern side is the Teatro Tomás Terry, built by sons of a wealthy plantation owner of that name. Caruso is among the great stars to have performed here. Opposite the cathedral is the Palacio Ferrer, built for another sugar millionaire and now the Casa de la Cultura, where concerts are held. The mansion's tower can be climbed for a fine view of the city. On the southern edge of the square stands the blue-balconied **Museo Provincial,** with a small collection exploring the city's history.

🍴 Unión ($), Avenida 54 y Calle 31

Museo Provincial

✉ Avenida 54, corner of Calle 27 ☎ (043) 51-9722 🕐 Tue–Sat 10–6, Sun 9–1 👆 Inexpensive

Central Cuba

CAYO SANTA MARÍA

Cayo Santa María is a set of islands off the north coast of Cuba in Villa Clara. Also known as La Cayería del Norte, this small cluster of cays are bordered by azure seas and dazzling white sands to the west. At their northern stretches the coast is wild and rocky. The least developed of the Cuban cays, there are currently only 10 hotel complexes here, reached by a 30-mile (50km) causeway (*pedraplén*). The most expensive, the Royal Hideaway Ensenachos,

actually sits on the cays' best beaches – the Playa Ensenachos and Playa Mégano. The least expensive, Villa Las Brujas, one of the few hotels in Cuba with a boutique feel, sits alongside the secluded curve of La Salina. While most people recline on the sands and bathe in the bathtub-warm sea, catamaran safaris and scuba diving are available from the marina next to Villa Las Brujas. The Barceló Cayo Santa María Beach Resort, a complex of four hotels, has opened El Pueblo, a faux Spanish colonial boulevard with multiple restaurants, a very attractive spa, bowling alley, disco and jazz club. A dolphinarium is also under construction.

➕ 14G

ℹ️ Marina Cayo Las Brujas; tel: (042) 35-0013

ESCAMBRAY MOUNTAINS

Best places to see, ➤ 42–43.

a drive through the Escambray Mountains

From the center of Trinidad (➤ 52–53), take Calle Prio Guinart, the main road toward Cienfuegos. After 2.5 miles (4km) turn right opposite the D'Prisa Toro bar toward Topes de Collantes and the Escambray Mountains (➤ 42–43).

The road to Topes de Collantes is stunning, the mountains rising to over 3,000ft (915m). The hillsides are cloaked in forests, but where the trees have been cleared there are coffee plantations. Topes de Collantes was created as a health resort; today the spa complex is for Cuban nationals only but the area is being developed for eco-tourism.

Beyond Topes, continue north on the very bad main road toward Manicaragua. The maximum speed along here is around 10mph (15kph).

The views over Lake Hanabanilla and the rolling foothills of Santa Clara province are stupendous as you snake downhill.

At Manicaragua, turn left for Cumanayagua, and then left again to reach the only hotel on the lake, Lago de Hanabanilla.

Explore the lake, waterfalls, restaurant and *campesino* home by boat from the hotel's dock.

After a night at the hotel, return to the main road and turn left to reach the main Trinidad–Cienfuegos coast road.

You'll pass through citrus orchards, with vistas of the Escambray to your left.

Turn right onto the main coast road and continue west to San Antón; turn left here for the beach resort of Rancho Luna for lunch. Return to San Antón and carry on to the small village of Pepito Tey, identified by its sugar-processing plant.

The comprehensive Soledad Botanical Gardens, opposite the entrance to Pepito Tey, are spread over 245 acres (99ha).

After exploring, continue to Cienfuegos or return along the coast road to Trinidad.

Distance 144 miles (232km)
Time 2 days
Start/end point Trinidad
➕ 11E
Lunch Hotel Rancho Luna ($$), Playa Rancho Luna, near Cienfuegos (➤ 161)
Accommodation
Hotel Hanabanilla (➤ 161)

JARDINES DEL REY

The islands of the Gardens of the King –
Cayo Coco and Cayo Guillermo – are two
large cays, joined to each other and the
mainland by a 17-mile (27km) causeway. Both
are fringed with stunning white sands and
turquoise seas. Cayo Guillermo is the smaller
of the two cays, home to just four hotels, a
marina and one of Cuba's most beautiful
beaches, Playa Pilar (▶ 67), an isolated thin
crescent blessed with honey sands, shallow
blue water and a rustic restaurant. It is named
after Ernest Hemingway's fishing boat, *Pilar*.
The writer favored deep-sea fishing off these
northern isles and Cayo Guillermo is
mentioned in his posthumously published
Islands in the Stream. The larger Cayo Coco
is more densely populated with hotels, but
this combined beach resort is low rise and
low density.

Around the islands are coral reefs, and
diving is popular; turtles can be seen in the
shallow water. Catamaran safaris also allow
snorkelers to see the tropical fish. Numerous
birds, including flamingos and white ibis, nest
in and around the mangroves that surround
the islands. To explore nature on land, visit the
ecological reserve of Parque Natural El Bagá,
near Laguna Redonda and Laguna de la
Leche, where fishing and boat tours are
possible. The Acavida Spa-Talaso offers
massage and mud therapy for those in search
of less active recreation.

✚ 15G

REMEDIOS

Remedios was founded in the early 16th century by Vasco Porcallo de Figueroa (who is said to have fathered over 200 children). Originally it stood on the coast, but frequent pirate raids forced townsfolk to move the settlement inland. Today it is one of the finest colonial towns on the island and famous as the venue for Cuba's most striking festival, the *Parrandas*. This started in the early 19th century when the local priest employed children to walk the streets on Christmas Eve, banging cans together to keep the population awake for midnight Mass. Soon the two districts *(barrios)* of the town were competing with each other to create the loudest noise. Today they build vast floats called

trabajos de plaza, although the floats are outdone in spectacle by the firework battles, accompanied by ear-splitting music. The festival offers a memorable, if noisy and sleepless night. Those who miss it can catch the flavor at the **Museo de las Parrandas,** devoted to its history.

On the main square, the **Church of San Juan Bautista** is

claimed by many to be the loveliest in Cuba. The altar, carved wood embellished with gold leaf, is by the artist Rogelio Atá. It was the gift of a rich benefactor in 1939. Close by are two small museums, one exploring the town's history (the Museo de Historia Local, at Calle Maceo 56). The other is the **Museo de Música Alejandro García Caturla.** Though a lawyer by profession, Caturla was also a composer whose influence on Cuban music was significant. His incorruptibility as a lawyer and his liberal views led to his murder in 1940, when he refused a leading politician's bribe.

✚ 12D 🍴 Hotel Mascotte ($$), Parque Martí; tel: (042) 39-5144

Museo de las Parrandas

✉ Calle Maximo Gómez 71
🕐 Tue–Sat 9–noon, 1–6, Sun 9–1
✋ Inexpensive

Church of San Juan Bautista

✉ Parque Martí

Museo de Música Alejandro García Caturla

✉ Parque Martí 5 🕐 Tue–Sat 9–noon, 1–5, Sun 9–1
✋ Inexpensive

SANCTI SPÍRITUS

After a visit in 1895, Winston Churchill recalled Sancti Spíritus as "a very second-rate place, and a most unhealthy place" *(My Early Life)*. Since Churchill's visit, the health of the town and its inhabitants has improved immeasurably, and though it is not in the first rank of tourist destinations, Sancti Spíritus deserves better than "second rate".

The town was one of the original seven *villas* (garrison towns) set up by Diego Velázquez in 1515 and the only one that was truly inland. The *villa* was moved after a few years, to a site on the Yayabo river. Though far from the sea, it was raided by pirates (and sacked twice) in the mid-17th century. In the years of peace that followed, the fertile lands that surrounded the town – and which now form the province of which Sancti Spíritus is the capital – supported vast sugar plantations that made their owners, and the town, rich. Sugar is still the most important local crop. The cane feeds the country's biggest sugar mill, while the cane trash is used to produce paper in a mill almost as large.

At the heart of the city is Parque Central (also called Parque Serafín Sánchez after a hero of the two Wars of Independence). The town church, the Iglesia del Espíritu Santo, lies a little way south. Declared a National Monument in 1978, it was built in the late 17th century on the foundations of a wooden church of 1522. The church tower was added in the 18th century and the cupola some 100 years later. The carved ceiling is claimed by many to be the finest on the island.

Closer to the square is the **Museo de Arte Colonial,** housed in a perfectly preserved 19th-century colonial mansion built for the Valle Iznaga family, at the time the most important family in the area. The mansion, with its beautiful courtyard, is superb. The furniture and furnishings form one of Cuba's best collections and include paintings, glassware and ceramics. The **Fundación de la Naturaleza y El Hombre** is full of anthropological miscellany relating to a 6,820-mile (10,975km) journey from the Amazon to Cuba by a team of Cubans. Facing the museum is the small yet charming Iglesia de Nuestra Señora de la Caridad church.

The Yayabo bridge is the only stone-arched bridge left on the island. The river it crosses has given its name to the *guayaba*, used to make the famous *guayabita* liqueur at Pinar del Río (➤ 134) and the *guayabera*, the loose-fitting shirt that was developed by workers from the town. Near the river, Calle Llano, another National Monument, is a winding, cobbled street with a collection of exquisite 19th-century houses. The Teatro Principal, also close to the bridge, is home to the *Coro de Claro,* a local choir that has achieved world renown.

✚ 13H 🍴 Mesón de la Plaza ($); ➤ 163

Museo de Arte Colonial

✉ Calle Plácido Sur 74 ☎ (041) 32-5455 🕔 Tue–Fri 9–5, Sat 2–8, Sun 8–noon 💵 Inexpensive

Fundación de la Naturaleza y El Hombre

✉ Calle Cruz Pérez, Parque de la Caridad ☎ (041) 32-8342 🕔 Mon–Fri 10–5 💵 Inexpensive

SANTA CLARA

Santa Clara is the capital of Villa Clara province – the most unspoilt of central Cuba's regions. The town was founded in the late 17th century by people who discovered that even the new inland village of Remedios (➤ 154–155) was not remote enough to ensure relief from pirate attack. Despite that early founding, Santa Clara does not have many rich colonial houses. It is, rather, a workmanlike place and an important industrial hub.

The town's position, almost at the heart of Cuba, has made it strategically important during the many battles for independence. Most famously, it was here that the decisive battle of the 1959 revolution was fought, with the victorious revolutionaries led by Che Guevara. On 28 December 1958 his handful of rebels attacked Santa Clara. When Che's men bulldozed a trainload of supplies sent by Batista to his beleaguered troops, the dictator realized that Santa Clara was lost; he resigned and fled on 1 January 1959. The remaining troops at Santa Clara surrendered the same day.

There is much in Santa Clara that commemorates the battle. The **Tren Blindado** is easily the most extraordinary memorial: the derailed trucks of the train (and the bulldozer, mounted on a plinth) have been preserved. The barracks where Batista's men surrendered is now the **Museo Provincial Abel Santamaría,** exploring the battle and other aspects of Santa Clara's history, as well as the natural history of Villa Clara province. In the Plaza de la Revolución is the Monumento Ernesto Che Guevara, with a mural of the battle and a massive statue of Che in battle dress, inscribed with that popular revolutionary slogan "Hasta la Victoria Siempre"– "Ever Onward to Victory". And perhaps most significantly, there is the small **Museo de Che**, filled with photos and memorabilia of the hero's life, and adjacent mausoleum inaugurated on 8 October 1997, when the bones of Che Guevara were brought back from Bolivia to rest in state at the site of his greatest triumph.

Of non-revolution Santa Clara, the best part is Parque Vidal (named for another revolutionary, Leoncio Vidal, who died in an earlier battle at the town, in 1896). On the square's northern edge is the fine, yellow-walled Teatro La Caridad with its ornate interior and, nearby, the **Museo de Artes Decorativas,** with a collection of colonial furnishings. At the square's southwestern corner, the

Hotel Libre maintains a bullet-marked facade, one more memorial to Che's battle. Five blocks northwest of Parque Vidal, the charming Plaza del Carmen hosts Iglesia Nuestra Señora del Carmen, a 17th-century church.

✚ 11D

Tren Blindado

✉ Calle Independencia 🕐 Mon–Sat 9–5:30 ✋ Inexpensive

Museo Provincial Abel Santamaría

✉ Calle Esquerra ☎ (042) 20-3041 🕐 Mon–Fri 8:30–5, Sat 9–1
✋ Inexpensive

Museo de Che

✉ Plaza de la Revolución ☎ (042) 20-5878 🕐 Tue–Sun 9–5:30 ✋ Free

Museo de Artes Decorativas

✉ Parque Vidal 27 ☎ (042) 20-5368 🕐 Mon–Thu 9–6, Fri 1–10, Sun 6–10
✋ Inexpensive

TRINIDAD

Best places to see, ➤ 52–53.

HOTELS

CIENFUEGOS
Jagua ($$–$$$)

One of the better hotels in central Cuba (built by Batista's brother in the 1950s). It may not be particularly characterful, but is well sited on the peninsula at the southern end of town, next to the Palacio del Valle and near Punta Gorda, with lovely views across the bay.

✉ Calle 37, 1, Cienfuegos ☎ (043) 55-1003

Rancho Luna ($$$)

Situated just a few steps from the area's best beach. Diving equipment can be rented and there are other sports facilities available. The rooms are air-conditioned and there is a restaurant and nightclub.

✉ Playa Rancho Luna, near Cienfuegos ☎ (043) 54-8012

ESCAMBRAY MOUNTAINS
Hanabanilla ($)

Your own transport is essential unless you are interested only in fishing, walking, horseback riding and the occasional boat trip. Beautifully sited, though the Soviet-style architecture is not aesthetically pleasing. The buffet diner is reasonable for such a remote spot and the refurbished rooms with international TV are extremely comfortable. The views from the rooftop bar are superb.

✉ Lake Hanabanilla in the Escambray Mountains ☎ (042) 20-8461

Los Helechos ($)

In the Topes de Collantes area, with a thermal swimming pool and access to the steam baths and gym at the Kurhotel spa. The rooms are pleasant and airy, and all have balconies. The cooler air will be welcomed by those wanting an active holiday in the Escambray Mountains, or a quiet respite from the sun and sand on the coast.

✉ Topes de Collantes ☎ (042) 54-0330

JARDINES DEL REY
Iberostar Daiquirí ($$$)
The best-managed resort on these northern cays, the Daiquirí sits on a lovely stretch of perfect, white-sand beach on Cayo Guillermo. There's a pool, well-tended gardens and a children's club, surrounded by low-key, ochre-colored Spanish colonial-style villas.
🖂 Cayo Guillermo, Jardines del Rey ☎ (033) 301-650; www.iberostar.com

REMEDIOS
Mascotte ($$)
The only hotel in town, situated in the main square and occupying a beautifully restored 19th-century building. Very atmospheric.
🖂 Parque Martí, Remedios ☎ (042) 39-5144

TRINIDAD
Iberostar Grand Hotel Trinidad ($$$)
Deluxe hotel – the best in the provinces – opened in 2006, with sumptuous accommodations, a gourmet restaurant, hip bar, games room and even an internet cafe.
🖂 Parque Céspedes ☎ (041) 99-6073

RESTAURANTS

CIENFUEGOS
Palacio del Valle ($$$)
See page 58.

Restaurante 1869 ($$)
Delightful period restaurant with elegant furnishings inside the attractive Hotel La Unión, serving some creative (although not always satisfying) dishes. The best restaurant in town.
🖂 Hotel Unión, Calle 31, e/ 54 y 56 ☎ (043) 55-1020 🕒 Daily 7–9:45am, noon–2:45pm, 7–9:45pm

ESCAMBRAY MOUNTAINS
El Río Negro ($$)
Romantically sited on the edge of the lake – the restaurant can only be reached by boat from the Hotel Hanabanilla – with

wonderful views, a very pleasant atmosphere and some excellent Cuban dishes.

✉ Lake Hanabanilla ☎ (042) 49-1125 🕐 Daily 10–6

SANCTI SPÍRITUS
Hostal Encanto del Ríjo ($$)

This hotel restaurant has a lovely colonial ambience and tasty, above-average fare. Try the garlic shrimp or roast chicken.

✉ Plaza Honorato ☎ (041) 32-8588 🕐 Daily 7am–10pm

Mesón de la Plaza ($)

One of the best provincial restaurants in Cuba, on a Spanish *bodega* theme. Serves a tremendous *garbanzo* (chickpea stew), plus grilled fish and meat dishes.

✉ Máximo Gómez 34, on Plaza Honorato ☎ (041) 32-8546 🕐 Daily 9am–11pm

SANTA CLARA
Hostal Florida Center ($–$$)

With the new wave of self-employment laws, flamboyant *casa particular* owner Angel Rodríguez has opened a *paladar* (private restaurant) on the gorgeous verdant patio of his colonial home. Dine alfresco on dishes such as shellfish, chicken fricasee or pork chop, accompanied by Cuban tunes. Reserving ahead is essential.

✉ Calle Maestra Nicolasa (Candelaria) 56, e/ Colón y Maceo ☎ (042) 20-8161 🕐 Daily 2–10

Paladar Sabor Latino ($$)

The only private restaurant in town serves filling *criollo* dishes in pleasant, clean surrounds.

✉ Esquerra 157 e/ Julio Jover y Berenguer ☎ (042) 20-6539
🕐 Daily noon–midnight

TRINIDAD
Iberostar Grand Hotel Trinidad ($$$)

Perhaps the most deluxe restaurant beyond Havana, this one

serves true gourmet fare that doesn't disappoint – a rarity in Cuba! Put on your best clothes.

✉ Parque Céspedes, in the Gran Hotel Iberostar Trinidad ☎ (041) 99-6073
🕑 Daily 12:30–3, 7–10

Sol y Son ($$)

This wonderful homespun *paladar* in the center of Trinidad has an interior filled with Spanish colonial furniture and a garden patio for comfortable alfresco dining. Alfredo, the maitre d', ensures the atmosphere is convivial and serves the house specialty, *ropa vieja* (shredded beef or lamb) and the local cocktail, *canchánchara*, with aplomb.

✉ Calle Simón Bolívar 283 e/ José Martí y Frank País, Trinidad ☎ (041) 99-2926 🕑 Daily 12:30–3, 7–late

Vía Real ($–$$)

Lovely little place with a wide-ranging menu from a sandwich or simple meal to an expensive lobster-based dinner.

✉ Plaza El Jigüe (Calle Martinez Villena esq Piro Guinart), Trinidad
☎ (041) 99-6476 🕑 Daily 10:30–10:30

ENTERTAINMENT

Casa de la Música, Trinidad
See page 62.

Club Benny Moré

In the heart of town, this small yet lively nightclub has excellent live performances (from *bolero* to jazz), followed by dancing.

✉ Avenida 54 e/ 29 y 31, Cienfuegos ☎ (043) 55-1674

El Mejunje

Cuba's most outré bar and entertainment venue is in the center of Santa Clara. Popular with the gay and transsexual community, it holds tranny nights on Saturdays (and sometimes even beauty shows), but the rest of the week there's a variety of entertainment, from heavy metal to salsa.

✉ Calle Marta Abreu 12, Santa Clara ☎ (042) 28-2572 🕑 Daily 10pm–late

Santiago de Cuba and Eastern Cuba

The east is the revolutionary heart of Cuba. Here the first war for independence from Spain began; here Fidel Castro first led rebels against Batista's forces; and here, after his imprisonment and exile, Castro landed with Che Guevara to start the conflict that led to Batista's overthrow.

Castro and his men hid in the mountains of the Sierra Maestra, Cuba's highest peaks, a paradise for walkers who are experienced enough to travel well off the beaten track. Beyond the mountains is Santiago de Cuba, once the island's capital and now its second city, with a wonderful center full of colonial buildings. On again is Guantánamo and the US Naval Base, a curious hangover of colonial rule. To the north is the coast where Columbus first landed in the New World. With its Amerindian sites and hidden colonial treasures, it is one of the most interesting areas of Cuba, and is probably still as beautiful as when Columbus first saw it.

Camagüey

Santiago de Cuba

SANTIAGO DE CUBA

One of the original seven Spanish settlements on Cuba, Santiago, founded in 1515, was soon made the island's capital, as its deep harbor was a natural base for the *conquistadores*. Santiago became a wealthy city, the discovery of copper in the hills to the west leading to rapid expansion. The city soon had to forfeit the status of capital to Havana, however, partly because it was prone to earthquakes, and partly because of the pirate raids that followed the increase in prosperity – Henry Morgan even sacked the city after the Morro fortress had been built.

At the end of the 18th century the slave revolt in Haiti led to a massive influx of French plantation owners. They brought with them their knowledge of sugar and coffee farming, and the rapid establishment of plantations led to a large number of slaves being shipped into Santiago. The French also brought their own culture, which, together with that of the African slaves, made cosmopolitan Santiago an evolutionary center of music and dance, best illustrated by Santiago's famous carnival in late July and its Festival del Caribe in early July. Those unable to make it to the carnival can sample its various aspects at the **Museo del Carnaval.**

Santiago's position in Cuba's various independence conflicts was critical. The black general Antonio Maceo, known as the "Bronze Titan" and a hero of both the Wars of Independence, was born in the city. And it was here that Castro made his first speech after Batista's flight, giving Santiago the title "Hero City".

✚ 21M

Museo del Carnaval

✉ Calle Heredia 303 ☎ (022) 62-6955 🕐 Tue–Sun 9–5
♿ Inexpensive

Castillo de San Pedro del Morro

This dramatic castle at the entrance to the bay was built in the mid-17th century to stop pirate raids on Santiago. It is one of the finest viewpoints on the island, with superb vistas to the Sierra Maestra. The castle hosts a *cañonazo* ceremony nightly at sunset, when soldiers in period costume fire a cannon, recalling a tradition that announced the closure of the harbor entrance.

✠ *Santiago de Cuba 1d (off map)* ✉ South of Santiago, near the airport
☎ (022) 69-1569 🕐 Daily 8–7:30 ✋ Inexpensive

Cuartel Moncada

It was in these barracks on 26 July 1953 that Castro launched his first attack against Batista's forces. The raid was a miserable failure, with many rebels being killed (or captured and executed). Castro himself was imprisoned but later amnestied due to public pressure. Today the barracks, the bullet-holed facade lovingly tended, houses a school and a museum of the revolution.

✚ Santiago de Cuba 4c ✉ Avenida Moncada ☎ (022) 62-1157 🕐 Tue–Sat 9:30–5, Sun 9:30–noon 👋 Inexpensive

Gran Piedra

A beautiful road heads east from Santiago toward the southern coast. After about 6 miles (10km) a road to the left ascends the Gran Piedra (Big Rock, 4,000ft/1,220m), an outlier of the Sierra Maestra. Close to the peak is a hotel/restaurant. From here 440 steps lead to the summit, crowned by the vast lump of rock that gives it its name. On clear days you can see Haiti and Jamaica. A short distance beyond the hotel is the **Cafetal La Isabelica,** the mansion of an old plantation, now a museum of plantation life.

✚ 21M ⊠ 12.5 miles (20km) west of Santiago 🚌 Taxi or tour bus only
Cafetal La Isabelica
✉ Gran Piedra ⏰ Daily 8–4 ✋ Inexpensive

Parque Baconao

The park covers an area of over 300sq miles (800sq km) and
includes a nature reserve, several good beaches and some
interesting tourist sites, including the Museo de la Guerra Hispano-
Americano, dedicated to the Spanish-American War. Nearby,
Granjita Siboney is the bullet-ridden farmhouse from where Fidel
and his troops set out to attack the Moncada barracks. A left turn
here leads to the **Valle de la Prehistória,** with its collection of life-
size concrete dinosaurs; and the Museo Nacional de Transporte
Terreste, displaying classic autos, including Benny Moré's flashy
gold Cadillac, and an impressive collection of toy cars. Farther
along is Acuario Baconao, a rather meager aquarium where
dolphins and sea lions perform.

✚ 21M ✉ About 28 miles (45km) west of Santiago 🚌 Taxi or tour bus only
Valle de la Prehistória
✉ Parque Baconao ☎ (022) 63-9239 ⏰ Daily 8–4:45 ✋ Inexpensive

Parque Céspedes

Best places to see, ➤ 48–49.

a walk around Santiago de Cuba

*From the cathedral in Parque Céspedes (▶ 48–49), head west along Calle Heredia, then turn first left along Calle Félix Peña. Turn third right along Calle Diego Palacios to reach the top of the steps on Calle Padre Pico. On the hill behind you is the **Museo de la Lucha Clandestina**.*

The museum tells the story of the urban guerillas who fought in the streets of Santiago during the revolution.

Walk down the steps and continue along Calle Pico to Calle Aguilera. Turn right, then first left. At the next intersection, turn right along Calle José Saco, Santiago's main shopping street (known as Enramadas).

Enramadas is fascinating, with its lively mix of shops.

*Follow the street to the Plaza de Marte, the **Museo de Ciencias Naturales Tomás Romay** is on the left.*

The museum has collections about natural history and archaeology, and some modern paintings.

Turn right along the square's western edge, then right again, following Calle Aguilera to Plaza de Dolores. Continue along the square's left-hand edge, then turn second left (Calle Rosado), passing the Museo Bacardí on the right.

Museo Bacardí was founded by rum baron Emilio Bacardí. It contains collections of weapons and paintings.

At the next intersection, the Museo del Carnaval (► 166) is to the left. Turn right and follow Calle Heredia, soon passing the Casa Natal de José Heredia to the left.

José María de Heredia, born in Santiago in 1803, is regarded as one of Latin America's finest poets.

Continue along Calle Heredia to return to Parque Céspedes.

Distance 2 miles (3km)
Time 1.5 hours; 4 hours with stops
Start/end point Parque Céspedes ✚ *Santiago de Cuba 2d*
Lunch Santiago 1900 ($$$); ► 184
Museo de la Lucha Clandestina
✉ Calle General Jesús Rabí 1 (top of Padre Pico steps) 🕐 Tue–Sun 9–5 💵 Inexpensive
Museo de Ciencias Naturales Tomás Romay
✉ Calle José Saco esq Barnada ☎ (022) 62-3277 🕐 Mon–Fri 8–5:30, Sat 8–2, Sun 2–5:30 💵 Inexpensive

Eastern Cuba

BARACOA
Best places to see,
➤ 36–37.

BAYAMO
Bayamo is the capital of the province of Granma, named after the boat that brought Castro, Guevara and the other 80 rebels to Cuba at the start of the revolution. Carlos Manuel de Céspedes, hero of Independence, was born in a house in the main square, now a museum devoted to him. His statue stands in the square and a plaque on the Ayuntamiento (Town Hall) recalls that here, in 1869, he signed a declaration abolishing slavery in "Free Cuba". Eventually forced from power by internal wranglings, Céspedes retired to nearby San Lorenzo to concentrate on his great passion, chess. Surprised by Spanish troops while contemplating a move at

the board, he declined to surrender and was shot dead. Beside the **Casa Natal** (birthplace museum) is the **Museo Provincial,** with items on the town's history, including the original score of Cuba's national anthem written by local poet Perucho Figueredo, whose bust can also be seen in Parque Céspedes.

✚ 19L ▮▮ Restaurant 1513 ($), Calle General Garcia 176

Casa Natal de Carlos Manuel de Céspedes

✉ Calle Maceo 57 (on west side of Parque Céspedes) ☎ (023) 42-3864
🕐 Tue–Fri 10–6, Sat–Sun 10–3, 8–10 ✋ Inexpensive

Museo Provincial

✉ Calle Maceo 55 ☎ (023) 42-4125 🕐 Tue–Sat 8–2, Sun 9–1
✋ Inexpensive

CAMAGÜEY

Camagüey was another of the seven garrison towns founded by Diego Velázquez. The first settlement was on the coast, and from it one of Velázquez' most vicious commanders, Lieutenant Narváez, raided an inland Amerindian village, killing all 2,000 inhabitants. Pirate attacks and mosquitoes forced the Spaniards to move inland. It is said that the site they moved to was the old Indian village and that Camagüey was the name of the slaughtered villagers' chieftain – although until 1903 the town was known as Santa María del Puerto del Príncipe. The town's layout was deliberately confusing to deter pirates.

The move failed however: the town was sacked by Henry Morgan in 1668 and again 10 years later by French pirate François

Granmont. But the townsfolk were determined to stay, the local land being good for both sugar and cattle. Today Camagüey lies in the heart of cattle country.

Although Camagüey is Cuba's third-largest city and has some fine colonial buildings and was declared a UNESCO World Heritage Site in 2008, it is rarely visited by tourists. This explains the poor state of some of its architecture, but is perhaps the reason that hustlers on bicycles attach themselves ferociously to tourists arriving in town.

As you walk around you are bound to pass one of the terra-cotta vessels called *tinajónes*. As the area is short of water, with few rivers and little rain, the townsfolk invented the *tinajón*, a huge pot into which the infrequent rainwater was guttered. Local legend has it that if a man drinks water offered to him by a woman from her *tinajón* he will stay with her in Camagüey for ever.

Not surprisingly for such a large city, Camagüey has its hero of the independence struggles. Ignacio Agramonte was born here in 1841 and led the local rebels during the First War of Independence. His birthplace, the **Casa Natal de Ignacio Agramonte,** is a museum dedicated to his memory.

The first church on the site of the **Catedral de Nuestra Señora de la Candelaria,** in Parque Agramonte, was built in 1530. The present building dates from the 19th century and contains some fine marble tombs and an impressive beamed ceiling.

North of the city center, near the railway station, the excellent **Museo Provincial** is housed in an old Spanish barracks.

Plaza de los Trabajadores (Square of the Workers) is notable for the lovely colonial church of **Nuestra Señora de la Merced,** a former convent church with a venerated image of the baby Jesus. The arched facade is delightful and inside are some superb 18th-century frescoes.

About the same distance from the Plaza, but to the northwest, the Teatro Principal is an impressive building with excellent stained glass and crystal chandeliers. The most exquisite plazas are the cobbled Plaza San Juan de Díos, surrounded by restored 18th-century homes and the Antiguo Hospital, or military hospital; and Plaza del Carmen, restored and unique for its life-size ceramic figures of actual citizens depicted in everyday situations.

✚ 16J

Casa Natal de Ignacio Agramonte

✉ Avenida Agramonte 459, Plaza de los Trabajadores ☎ (032) 29-7116 🕐 Tue–Sat 9–5 ✋ Inexpensive

Catedral de Nuestra Señora de la Candelaria

✉ Calle Cisneros esq Luaces ☎ (032) 29-4965

Museo Provincial Ignacio Agramonte

✉ Avenida de los Mártires 2 esq Calle Ignacio Sánchez ☎ (032) 28-2425 🕐 Tue–Sat 10–1, 2–5, Sun 10–1 ✋ Inexpensive

Nuestra Señora de la Merced

✉ Plaza de los Trabajadores ☎ (032) 29-2783

EL COBRE

Best places to see, ➤ 40–41.

GIBARA

Gibara is an untouristy fishing town on the north coast, also known as Villa Blanca (White Town) for its former whitewashed colonial buildings. It overlooks a bay and is hemmed in by the Silla de Gibara, a noticeably flat-topped mountain visible from all around. The 19th-century San Fulgencio church dominates the main plaza. A short walk away is the handsome Museo de Artes Decorativas (currently closed to repair hurricane damage). Gibara is famous for the Festival Internacional del Cine Pobre held each April. It was inaugurated by the late film director Humberto Solás and screens low-budget movies.

✚ 20K

GUANTÁNAMO

The US naval base, the reason most visitors have heard of Guantánamo, cannot be seen from the town, which itself has little of the colonial splendor of other Cuban towns, though the Parque Martí and the pretty church of Santa Catalina de Riccis that stands on it, are worth a look. The Mirador de Malones, a viewing platform from where you could see the naval base, has been closed for some time, but you can see the base from the rooms of the Hotel Cainamera.

✚ 22L

GUARDALAVACA

Guardalavaca is the collective name for a group of secluded beach resorts on Cuba's northeastern coast. The name translates as "watch the cow," and reflects the pastoral idyll this area encapsulates. Rolling hills and clusters of royal palms tumble down

toward a sea of deep turquoise blue studded with evergreen. The coastline is also peppered with small coves and isolated beaches, some of which belong to the handful of resorts. The main Guardalavaca beach area has two principal resorts, with a larger one planned. Farther west are Playa Yuraguanal, Playa Esmeralda and Playa Pesquero, each with one or two large beach resorts. Diving, sailing and especially snorkeling are popular, as the waters are shallow for miles and the views are beautiful.

✚ 21K

HOLGUÍN

Cuba's fourth city is the capital of one of the island's most beautiful and richest provinces, with a prosperous sugar industry and nickel and cobalt mines. Columbus probably landed here, and Fidel Castro's father was one of the area's wealthiest farmers.

Holguín has a center notable for the number of squares, the most important of which is Parque Calixto García, named for a local hero of the Wars of Independence. On the northern edge of the square, the **Museo de História Provincial** is housed in an old mansion used as barracks by the Spanish and known as La Periquera (the Parrot Cage) since the brightly uniformed Spaniards were besieged in it for two months by local insurgents during the First War of Independence. The museum has one of Cuba's best pre-Columbian collections, including an Amerindian stone axe carved in the shape of a man. Across the square is a natural history mueum, **Museo de Ciencias Naturales.**

At the north end of Holguín the Loma de la Cruz (Hill of the Cross) is a place of pilgrimage, following a vision of the Virgin in 1790. Pilgrims climb 468 steps, but visitors can use a road to reach the panoramic view from the summit.

North of Holguín, at Bariay Bay near Gibara, a monument marks the spot where, it is believed, Columbus first landed in the Americas. To the east is the beach resort of Guardalavaca (► 176–177).

South of Guardalavaca, at Banes (where Fidel Castro was married in 1948) is the **Museo Indocubano,** one of Cuba's most important Amerindian museums. Some of the artefacts in the museum were excavated from the **Chorro de Maíta** Taíno Indian burial site, nearby. At Birán, southeast of Holguín, Fidel Castro's birthplace at Finca Manacas is open to the public. The former rural estate of his father, now called **Sitio Histórico Birán,** includes many items from Fidel's early life.
✚ 20K

Museo de História Provincial
✉ Parque Calixto García ☎ (024) 46-3395 🕓 Tue–Sat 9–4:30, Sun 8:30–noon 💷 Inexpensive

Museo de Ciencias Naturales
✉ Calle Maceo 129 e/ Martí y Luz Caballero ☎ (024) 42-3935 🕓 Tue–Sat 9am–10pm, Sun 9–9 💷 Inexpensive

Museo Indocubano
✉ Calle General Marrero 305, Banes ☎ (024) 80-2487 🕓 Tue–Sat 9–5, Sun 8–noon 💷 Inexpensive

Chorro de Maíta
✉ South of the village of Yaguajay, 4 miles (6.5km) east of Guardalavaca ☎ (024) 43-0201 🕓 Daily 9–5 💷 Inexpensive

Sitio Histórico Birán
✉ Birán, 37 miles (60km) southeast of Holguín ☎ (024) 28-6102 🕓 Tue–Sat 9–4, Sun 9–noon 💷 Moderate

a drive through Granma province

Start early so you can be sure to reach Niquero before nightfall. Head 33 miles (53km) west out of Bayamo to Manzanillo, then take the coast road that runs southwest of Manzanillo along the the finger of land that juts out into the Caribbean. After 8 miles (13km) you will reach the remains of the sugar plantation of Carlos Manuel de Céspedes at **La Demajagua.**

Céspedes, a *criollo* (Spaniard born in Cuba), was the first to free his slaves in 1868, thereby launching the First War of Independence (from Spain) on 10 October 1868.

Continue 17 miles (27km) to Media Luna, home of the Museo Celia Sánchez.

Sánchez, a key female rebel in the 1959 revolution, was also Fidel Castro's personal secretary.

Continue 14 miles (23km) to the town of Niquero and stay here overnight. From here it is another 8 miles (13km) farther south to explore Parque Nacional Desembarco del Granma.

The park marks the spot where Castro and his band of rebels landed to ignite the revolution in 1956. A wooden walkway is carved into the mangroves, and there is a model of the *Granma* and a small museum. The El Guafe trail nearby takes you to carved Indian idols in caves, and there are many other trails in the park.

From Niquero, head 23.5 miles (38km) southeast to Pilón, on the south coast. The road from here to Santiago (108.5 miles/175km) is a spectacular drive. The journey will take 5–6 hours as the road cannot be taken at speed.

The road hugs the coastal landscape at the edge of the Sierra Mountains as the luscious forest tumbles down to the sea. After hurricanes have tunneled through, parts of the road may be damaged, so it is important to seek advice in Pilón before setting off to Santiago.

After 66 miles (107km) stop in Chivirico at the tiny hotel on a peak, Los Galeones, to eat and admire the view, framed in bougainvillea, before the last stretch to Santiago.

Distance 204 miles (328km)
Time 2 days
Start point Bayamo ✚ 19L
End point Santiago de Cuba ✚ 21M
Lunch Brisas Sierra Mar Los Galeones, Playa Sevilla; tel: (022) 32-9110
Accommodation Hotel Niquero, Calle Martí 100 e/ Céspedes y 2 de Diciembre, Niquero; tel: (023) 59-2367
La Demajagua
🕐 Mon–Sat 8–5, Sun 8–1 💵 Inexpensive
Museo Celia Sánchez
🕐 Tue–Sun 9–5 💵 Free
Parque Nacional Desembarco del Granma
🕐 Daily 7–6 💵 Moderate

HOTELS

BARACOA
El Castillo ($$)
Irresistible hotel in an 18th-century clifftop fort with wonderful views of the town and El Yunque from the pool terrace. The elevated position adds a little air to the hottest of days and is very pleasant in the evenings.
✉ Calle Calixto García, Baracoa ☎ (021) 64-5194

BAYAMO
Hotel Royalton ($–$$)
Well situated on the main square, this renovated, mid-range Encanto hotel is comfortable and has modest amenities, including a simple restaurant.
✉ Maceo 53, Parque Céspedes, Bayamo ☎ (023) 42-2246

CAMAGÜEY
Gran Hotel ($$)
Not as grand as the name, but very comfortable. Within easy reach of the middle of town and with a good fifth-floor restaurant that offers a superb view.
✉ Calle Maceo 64 e/ Agramonte y Gómez, Camagüey ☎ (032) 29-2093

HOLGUÍN
Brisas Guardalavaca ($$$)
An attractive, all-inclusive resort hotel on a beautiful stretch of beach. Excellent facilities including water-sports equipment hire, tennis and horseback riding: especially good for families with children. Several fine restaurants and a nightly disco.
✉ Playa Guardalavaca ☎ (024) 43-0218

Sol Río de Luna y Mares ($$$)
Architecturally interesting resort built around large swimming pools just a few steps from the beach. Sports and diving facilities, and diving tuition and certification.
✉ Playa Esmeralda, about 4 miles (6km) southwest of Guardalavaca
☎ (024) 43-0060

PLAYA SEVILLA
Brisas Sierra Mar Los Galoones ($$$)
All-inclusive resort, magically sited on a hillside terrace with its own beach. Numerous sports facilities and free loan of water-sports equipment. The ultimate in luxury. There is a second, related, smaller resort nearby – Los Galeones – which is much smaller and perched on a rocky bluff. The facilities of Sierra Mar are available to guests at Los Galeones.

✉ Playa Sevilla, about 43 miles (70km) southwest of Santiago de Cuba

☎ (022) 32-9110; www.hotelescubanacan.com

SANTIAGO DE CUBA
Hotel Casa Grande ($$$)
Elegant hotel overlooking Santiago's main square. The elegance extends to the rooms and furnishings, making it one of the best places to stay while exploring the city. It has an excellent restaurant and a popular patio snack bar.

✉ Parque Céspedes, Santiago de Cuba ☎ (022) 65-3021

Meliá Santiago de Cuba ($$$)
The most luxurious hotel in town, but a little away from the center. The view from the Bello Bar on the 15th floor is superb. Well-appointed rooms and good buffet-style meals.

✉ Avenida de Las Américas esq Calle M, Santiago de Cuba ☎ (022) 68-7070

RESTAURANTS

BARACOA
Duaba ($–$$)
Elegant restaurant in the old fortress hotel. Serves creative regional cuisine using coconut as a base. Some of the most delicious food on the island.

✉ In the Hotel El Castillo ☎ (021) 64-5106 🕐 Daily 7am–10pm

Paladar La Colonial ($$)
The only *paladar* in Baracoa. Spacious home filled with antiques. Filling seafood and *criollo* food are served.

✉ Martí 123 e/ Maraví y Frank País ☎ (021) 64-5391 🕐 Daily 11–11

BAYAMO
La Sevillana ($$)
An elegant Spanish *bodega* (and the *only* nice eatery in town).
Garbanzo, plus chicken with wine are recommended, washed
down with sangría. Bring a sweater against the chill air-
conditioning.
✉ Calixto García e/ Figueredo y Lora ☎ (023) 42-1462 🕐 Daily noon–11

CAMAGÜEY
Salon Caribé ($)
The Gran Hotel has one of the best restaurants in town and its
fifth-floor position adds a superb view to the good food from a
reasonable menu.
✉ Calle Maceo 64 e/ Agramonte y Gómez, Camagüey ☎ (032) 29-2314
🕐 Daily noon–3, 7–10

HOLGUÍN
1720 Las Parques ($$)
This restaurant is the best in town, with a fine Cuban menu and
excellent food, usually including a good range of vegetables.
✉ Frexes e/ Manduley y Miró, Holguín ☎ (024) 45-8150 🕐 noon–10:30

SANTIAGO DE CUBA
Hotel Casa Grande ($$$)
The ground-floor restaurant overlooking Santiago's main square
serves excellent food. After your meal, take a drink in the roof
garden bar for a marvellous view of the city.
✉ Parque Céspedes, Santiago de Cuba ☎ (022) 65-3021 🕐 7–10, noon–3,
7:30–10

Restaurante El Morro ($$)
See page 59.

Santiago 1900 ($$$)
A training center for chefs, and the best restaurant in Santiago.
Situated on the patio of a Bacardí family mansion that is beautifully
furnished, with huge chandeliers. Cuban and international menu.

✉ Calle Bartolomé Masó 354 e/ Pio Rosado y Hartmann, Santiago de Cuba
☎ (022) 62-3507 🕓 Daily noon–midnight

ZunZún ($$$)

To the east of the Hotel Santiago, a little way from the centre. In a delightful colonial mansion, it offers a good menu and well-prepared meals.

✉ Avenida Manduley 159, Santiago de Cuba ☎ (022) 64-1528 🕓 Daily noon–10

ENTERTAINMENT

Bello Bar

Elegant bar and fine views – the perfect cocktail spot. There's also a live show every evening.

✉ Hotel Santiago, Avenida Américas esq Calle M, Santiago de Cuba
☎ (022) 687070 ❓ Dress code

Caberet Nocturno

Small-scale yet sexy cabaret followed by a disco, popular with local couples on weekends.

✉ Carretera Central, Holguín ☎ (024) 42-9345

Club El Iris

Loud, sweaty, packed. This is the most popular disco in town.

✉ Aguilera 617, near Plaza de Marte, Santiago de Cuba ☎ (022) 65-4910

Santiago Café

Themed as a colonial village, this trendy nightspot has live bands and a small cabaret followed by a disco.

✉ Hotel Santiago, Avenida Américas esq Calle M, Santiago de Cuba
☎ (022) 68-7070

Tropicana

Second only to the Tropicana in Havana, this outdoor cabaret is Caribbean themed.

✉ On the Autopista Nacional, 1.2 miles (2km) from the center of Santiago
☎ (022) 64-2579

Index

Acknowledgements

The Automobile Association would like to thank the following photographers, companies and picture libraries for their assistance in the preparation of this book.

Abbreviations for the picture credits are as follows – (t) top; (b) bottom; (c) centre; (l) left; (r) right; (AA) AA World Travel Library.

4l Playa Ancon, AA/D Henley; **4c** Jose Marti Airport, AA/C Sawyer; **4r** Varadero beach scene, AA/D Henley; **5l** Cienfuegos, AA/C Sawyer; **5c** Marina Hemingway, Havana, AA/C Sawyer; **6/7** Playa Ancon AA/D Henley; **8/9** Sierra Escambray AA/D Henley; **10cl** Cowboy AA/D Henley; **10/11t** Cubans AA/C Sawyer; **10/11b** Playa Girón AA/D Henley; **11tl** Tobacco fields AA/C Sawyer; **11tcl** American car AA/C Sawyer; **11cl** Fidel poster AA/D Henley; **12bl** Camagüey market AA/C Sawyer; **12cr** Street vendor AA/C Sawyer; **13** Roast pig AA/C Sawyer; **14t** Street delivery AA/C Sawyer; **14bl** Ice cream AA/C Sawyer; **15t** Street vendor AA/C Sawyer; **15c** Rum AA/C Sawyer; **15b** Market scene AA/C Sawyer; **16bl** Mural AA/D Henley; **16bc** Hemingway statue AA/D Henley; **16/17** Musicians AA/C Sawyer; **17br** Cigars AA/C Sawyer; **18** Playa Girón AA/D Henley; **19t** Ice-cream parlor AA/C Sawyer; **19c** Souvenirs AA/D Henley; **19b** Restored building AA/C Sawyer; **20/21** José Martí Airport AA/C Sawyer; **23cl** Goat cart AA/D Henley; **25** May Day, © Roberto Fumagalli/Alamy; **26cl** Airport AA/C Sawyer; **30cr** Mail box AA/D Henley; **30bl** Telephone, Claire Boobbyer; **34/35** Beach scene AA/D Henley; **36/37** Bay of Baracoa, Claire Boobbyer; **38** Catedral AA/D Henley; **38/39** Plaza de la Catedral AA/D Henley; **39** Catedral AA/D Henley; **40t** Interior AA/D Henley; **41** El Cobre AA/C Sawyer; **42cl** Escambray Mountains AA/C Sawyer; **42bl** National flower AA/D Henley; **43** Waterfall AA/D Henley; **44/45b** Boys fishing AA/D Henley; **45tr** Restored building AA/C Sawyer; **46cl** Museo de la Revolución AA/C Sawyer; **46/47** Interior AA/D Henley; **47tr** Painting of Castro's victory in Revolution, Museum of the Revolution, © Michael Honegger/Alamy; **48/49t** Parque Céspedes AA/C Sawyer; **48/49b** Parque Cespedes, © Melvyn Longhurst/Alamy; **50cl** Banana flower AA/D Henley; **51tr** Ox cart AA/D Henley; **50/51b** Lake AA/D Henley; **52/53** Trinidad rooftops, Claire Boobbyer; **53** Bass player, Trinidad de Cuba, Photolibrary; **54b** Farmer AA/C Sawyer; **54/55t** Karst outcrop AA/D Henley; **56/57** The Prado AA/C Sawyer; **59** La Terraza, Photolibrary; **60/61** Beach AA/D Henley; **62/63** Dancers, Sabado de la Rumba, Claire Boobbyer; **64/65** Old Havana AA/D Henley; **66/67** Varadero beach, © mediacolor's/Alamy; **69** Dolphin AA/C Sawyer; **70/71** Beach AA/D Henley; **72/73** Marina Hemingway AA/C Sawyer; **75bl** Toward the Museo de la Revolución AA/D Henley; **76/77** La Bodeguita del Medio, AA/C Sawyer; **78/79** Calle Obispo AA/C Sawyer; **79** Traditional pharmacy, Taquechel, on Calle Obispo, © John Warburton-Lee Photography/Alamy; **80/81b** Capitolio Nacional AA/C Sawyer; **81cl** Casa de África AA/C Sawyer; **82/83** Castillo de la Real Fuerza AA/C Sawyer; **83br** Plaza de la Catedral AA/D Henley; **84** Rolls Royce mascot, Despósito del Automóvil, Claire Boobbyer; **85t** Partagás tobacco factory AA/C Sawyer; **86** Hotel Ambos Mundos AA/D Henley; **88/89** Revolutionary Museum, Granma Memorial, © allOver photography/Alamy; **91** Street vendor AA/C Sawyer; **92** Restored building AA/D Henley; **93tr** Plaza de Armas courtyard AA/D Henley; **94** Plaza de la Catedral AA/D Henley; **95** Catedral de la Habana, AA/C Sawyer; **96/97b** Cementerio de Colón AA/C Sawyer; **98** Cojimar, Hemingway statue, AA/D Henley; **99** Torreon de Cojimar, AA/D Henley; **100** Santeria objects AA/C Sawyer; **100/101** Hotel Nacional AA/C Sawyer; **102/103** La Cabaña AA/C Sawyer; **104** Museo de Artes Decorativas AA/C Sawyer; **104/105** Interior AA/C Sawyer; **106/107** Napoleon museum, Claire Boobbyer; **108/109** Obelisk AA/C Sawyer; **109** Dancers at Tropicana Cabaret, Photolibrary; **111** Parque Lenin AA/C Sawyer; **117** Guanahacabibes AA/D Henley; **118** Billboard AA/C Sawyer; **118/119** Catedral AA/D Henley; **120** Museo Farmacéutico AA/C Sawyer; **121** Plaza de la Vigía, Matanzas, Claire Boobbyer; **122** Teatro Sauto, AA/D Henley; **122/123** Cuevas de los Pesces AA/D Henley; **124/125** Catedral AA/D Henley; **125t** Christopher Columbus AA/D Henley; **125bl** Horse and carriage AA/D Henley; **126/127** The Canarreos AA/D Henley; **129** Zapata Peninsula AA/C Sawyer; **130/131** Isla de la Juventud AA/D Henley; **131t** Rural housing AA/D Henley; **131b** Sorting corn AA/D Henley; **132/133** Guanahacabibes, AA/C Sawyer; **134/135** Catedral de San Rosendo AA/D Henley; **136** Natural History Museum AA/D Henley; **137** Hand-rolling tobacco AA/C Sawyer; **138** Flowers AA/D Henley; **138/139** Waterfall AA/D Henley; **145** Mule AA/D Henley; **146/147t** Castillo de Jagua village AA/D Henley; **146/147b** Palacio del Valle AA/D Henley; **148** Parque Marti AA/D Henley; **148/149** Cayo Santa Maria, © Alain Machet (4)/Alamy; **150/151** Sierra Escambray AA/C Sawyer; **152/153** Cayo Guillermo, Claire Boobbyer; **154t** Remedios AA/D Henley; **154bl** San Juan Bautista AA/D Henley; **154/155** Church interior AA/D Henley; **156/157** Sancti Spiritus AA/D Henley; **158/159** Parque Vidal AA/C Sawyer; **160** Santa Clara AA/D Henley; **165** El Cobre AA/D Henley; **166** Plaza de la Revolución AA/D Henley; **166/167** El Morro fortress AA/D Henley; **168** Moncada Barracks AA/C Sawyer; **169** Valle de la Prehistoria AA/D Henley; **170** Museo Bacardí AA/D Henley; **172l** Capilla de la Dolorosa AA/D Henley; **172/173t** Classical housing AA/D Henley; **173br** Government food store AA/D Henley; **174/175** Tinajones AA/D Henley; **176** Gibara church and town, Claire Boobbyer; **176/177** Guardalavaca, Photolibrary; **178b** Holguin AA/D Henley; **178/179t** Catedral de San Isidoro AA/D Henley; **180** Southern coastal road, Claire Boobbyer

Every effort has been made to trace the copyright holders, and we apologise in advance for any unintentional omissions or errors. We would be pleased to apply any corrections in a following edition of this publication.

Sight locator index

This index relates to the maps on the covers. We have given map references to the main sights of interest in the book. Grid references in italics indicate sights featured on town plans. Some sights within towns may not be plotted on the maps.